THE SEVEN STEPS
TO
PERSONAL SAFETY

The Seven Steps to Personal Safety

How to Avoid, Deal With, or Survive the Aftermath of
a Violent Confrontation

Richard B. Isaacs, M.A.

Tim Powers

Illustrated by D. F. Bach

The program described in this book is approved by the ASR Instructors Council.
This book is not intended to replace a training program approved by a
manufacturer of any self-defense item.

The Center for Personal Defense Studies
New York, New York

Published by
The Center for Personal Defense Studies
P.O. Box 2464, New York NY 10009-8921.

Copyright © 1993 by Stephen L. Isaacs

Library of Congress
Catalog Card Number: 93-90239
ISBN 1-883633-00-1
ISBN 1-883633-01-X (pbk.)

Design by Catherine Nicodemo
Illustration by D. F. Bach

For information or to order, address:
The Center for Personal Defense Studies
c/o The Seven Steps
P.O. Box 1225, Brookline MA 02146-0010.

Manufactured in the United States of America.

First Edition   1 2 3 4 5 6 7 8 9 0

Thou preparest a shield before me
in the presence of my enemies
23rd Psalm

TABLE OF CONTENTS

HOW TO AVOID
A VIOLENT CONFRONTATION

HOW TO SURVIVE THE AFTERMATH OF A VIOLENT CONFRONTATION

STEP 6
IMMEDIATELY NOTIFY THE POLICE OF THE ATTACK   139

STEP 7
DEAL WITH THE POST-TRAUMATIC STRESS OF BEING ASSAULTED   149

WHY WE WROTE THIS BOOK
AND HOW IT WILL KEEP YOU SAFE

We, the authors of this book, have invested much of our adult lives in trying to understand violence. We've felt the horror, terror, and anguish that violence causes. We've seen the needless suffering of innocent people who could have avoided or escaped a violent situation with just a little knowledge and preparation.

Violence has become more intrusive year after year in this country. While the police do their best, it's their job to enforce the laws *of* the state *for* the state. And while it comes as a shock to most of us, it is *not* the job of law enforcement agencies to protect us from harm. It is, therefore, up to each of us to take firsthand action to ensure our, and our family's, personal safety. This does not mean taking the law into our own hands. It does mean developing our own knowledge, techniques, tactics, and strategies to guard against being the needless subject of violence.

The focus of this book, therefore, is on *awareness* and *avoidance*. It is directed toward those who are aware that there is some potential for "bad things" to happen in this world, and who would like to know the options involved in balancing freedom and safety—particularly since these options are minor and non-intrusive, much the way wearing a seatbelt is a minor inconvenience when contemplating the alternatives in once-in-a-lifetime automobile accident.

Our primary goal is to teach you to *avoid* conflict; however we will also deal with what to do if all preventive efforts fail and you're confronted by an actual attack, as well as what you should do after you have survived a confrontation.

We hope you will read this entire book cover to cover before you implement the strategies, tactics, and techniques we present for your consideration.

Understanding the Present Threat

Most people have a fairly accurate view of the relative danger and safety of their lives. But some people, when looking at the potential danger, take the attitude that "It will never happen to me," or say that "If it's going to happen then it's going to happen," or think "I just don't have enough time to take precautions." In most cases it's not a question of risk, fate, or time: They just don't use common sense in taking the minimal precautions that would allow them to avoid, get away from, or survive the aftermath of a violent confrontation.

If it ever happens, will you be prepared? Will you have a plan of action? Will you have done everything you could to ensure your personal defense and safety?

A Continuum of Plans and Strategies for Personal Defense Safety

Our business is to analyze violence, and to develop plans and strategies to lessen or eliminate danger. As professionals committed to developing improved safety techniques, we constantly look for and try out new ideas and options that will effectively get that job done for you, independent of your age, your sex, your size, your strength, or your athletic ability. And when we find something that works, we add it to our repertoire.

Understand that there is no magic way of avoiding being the subject of violence, and that nothing is 100% effective when dealing with the unpredictability of human behavior. Human behavior—yours and your attacker's—cannot be predicted with any degree of certainty, especially in a crisis situation, so we are quick to concede that no technique is 100% effective every time for every person in every situation.

In the final analysis, you have to do the best you can with the options available to you, and the more options you have, the greater your chance for survival. We can't say to you that our suggestions will always work. We can only say that—based on our expertise, training, and experience—the procedures outlined in *The Seven Steps to Personal Safety* are realistic, effective, and practical. They have stood the test of time and are still standing.

A Systems Approach to Personal Defense and Safety

In designing a plan of positive action, we try to think of everything that can happen before, during, and after a violent confrontation. Then we design and test a series of plans for avoiding and dealing with these events and behaviors. This type of planning is called *when/then* thinking: *when* this happens, *then* I will do that; *when* that happens, *then* I will do this.

The key is to know clearly what your objectives are. Your objectives are to *avoid* being assaulted in the first place, to *get away* safely if you are assaulted, and to *survive* the aftermath if you can't get away. To achieve these objectives, you will need a series of options that give you the ability to change your personal defense plan as circumstances change. The more options you have at your disposal, the greater your chance for survival.

Not every option presented here will be appropriate for every person in every situation. But, taken as a whole, these options are intended to be effective whether you are an agile teenager or an octogenarian, a dancer or someone in a wheelchair. In addition, even though the techniques and scenarios discussed in this book show avoidance and defense strategies against one assailant, all are designed to work against more than one attacker, handling the most dangerous first, then the next, then the next. . .

America is the greatest country on Earth. It is also one of the more violent.[1] Dr. Peter DiVasto posits that this may be a result of long-term post-violence stress disorder resulting from the American experience in the Civil War, and since institutionalized within our culture. Whatever the reasons, if we are going to stay here in the midst of the violence, let's do something about it!!!

The Seven Steps to Personal Safety will allow you to be more aware of your surroundings, more prudent when appropriate, and to weave a system of personal defense and safety into the fabric of your everyday life. You will learn how to gradually modify your daily behavior to reduce opportunities for anyone to assault you.

These changes in behavior should change your attitude toward life in general, but the changes shouldn't be toward a negative paranoia. Instead, since they help keep you safer and feeling more in control, they should result in an increase in self-assurance and a renewed appreciation for the good things in life.

The following Seven Steps to Personal Safety flow naturally from one to the next. The initial four steps are the ranking priorities: avoiding confrontation. The next step helps you deal with the

---

1. According to Taylor Buckner of Concordia University, even if you exclude all gun deaths the United States still has a homicide rate two and one-half times higher than Canada.

worst-case scenario of an assault. The last two steps deal with the aftermath of being assaulted.

The Seven Steps to Personal Safety

Step 1
Be aware of your vulnerability.

Step 2
Mentally commit to doing everything you can
to stay safe.

Step 3
Be aware of your environment
and take reasonable precautions.

Step 4
Get away by creating and maintaining distance.

Step 5
Stop the assault and then get away.

Step 6
Immediately notify law enforcement authorities
of the attack.

Step 7
Deal with the post-traumatic stress
of being assaulted.

Best wishes and be safe,

Richard B. Isaacs
New York City, New York

Tim Powers
New London, Wisconsin

How to Avoid a Violent Confrontation

BE AWARE OF YOUR VULNERABILITY

STEP 1
BE AWARE OF YOUR VULNERABILITY

Most of us are concerned about our personal safety and the personal safety of our loved ones. The big question is how we can live in safety, free of confrontation and stress, and, failing that, how we can protect ourselves. To a large extent your first priority should be to judge how much potential danger you really face, and then decide what *reasonable* and *prudent* steps you should take to avoid or deal with this level of potential danger.

On first blush it would appear that violence has escalated tremendously, and is totally out of control throughout the country. Both newspapers and television news broadcasts are filled, daily, with horrible acts of senseless violence guaranteed to scare any thinking person, and senseless violence has become the staple of television and the movies. The National Institute of Justice released statistics in 1991 which indicate that every U.S. citizen has an 83% chance of being violently assaulted at least once in his or her lifetime, and that five out of every six of today's 12-year-old children will be the subject of violence (rape, murder, or robbery) sometime during their lives, and that half of these will face violence twice.

This certainly inclines us to believe that violence is everywhere, and, to a large extent, your analysis of risk will be determined by a combination of what you see in newspapers and on television, and by whether you know people who have been assaulted, or have been assaulted yourself. In general, your gut feelings will be a fairly accurate assessment of the risk you take.

On the other hand, it is clear that reporting of violence is much better and more active than ever before. Because of this, it is important that we carefully examine the appropriate statistics to find out what is really going on: Is there more violence, or merely more reported violence.

In fact, according to "Criminal Victimization 1991" (*Bureau of Justice Statistics Bulletin*, October 1992) in 1981 about 6.6 million violent incidents occurred, while there were about 6.4 million violent incidents in 1991. These figures are taken for the country as a whole, but vary widely according to where you live, work, and play. We know intuitively that the average suburbanite is more at risk than the average rural dweller, that the average urban dweller is more at risk than the average suburbanite, and that the average inner-city dweller faces the greatest risk of all. According to "Criminal Victimization 1991," Blacks are more likely than other races to be the subject of violence. Persons under 25 are more likely to be the subject of violence than older persons. Those living in households at the lowest income levels are more likely to be the subject of violence than those from households in the higher income brackets. Violence rates are highest in the West and South, and lowest in the Northeast.[2]

While these relationships are for all kinds of violence, they are certainly in line with other statistics which indicate that homicide rates have been falling for decades for every group except inner-city teenage males.

Unfortunately, there will always be *some* risk in your life, no matter who you are, where you live, or what you do. This is because we all do a lot of different things in a lot of different places. Some of these things are riskier than others, and some of these places are more dangerous than others.

And where are the police during all this? Well, assume for the moment that there are about 600,000 police officers in the United States. Of

---

2. Note that one ought to take the more frightening figures with a grain of salt. We have heard of, but not seen, two studies which indicated that huge numbers of children have been the victim of childhood sexual abuse (62%) and incest (19%). These studies supposedly defined "children" to be as old as 18. "Sexual abuse" was sufficiently loosely defined as to include suggestive remarks between 17-year-olds. "Incest" could include a one-time voluntary passionate kiss between a 13-year-old and her second cousin's 19-year-old stepbrother, or a voluntary long-term relationship between a 17-year-old and a distantly related 22-year-old. Poorly drawn studies trivialize serious problems.

these, 10% are administrative and another 10% are detectives. This leaves 480,000. Assuming three shifts, 160,000 police are potentially on duty at any time. Now factor in vacations and sick time, and you have well under 150,000 police officers on patrol throughout the country at any given time, or more than 1,300 people for each officer on street duty. Clearly, with the police spread this thin, each of us has to take responsibility for his or her own protection.

The good news is that, even in the '90s, less than 10% of all felonies committed are classified as being against the person. And even though there is some statistical possibility that you may be violently assaulted sometime in your life, this doesn't warrant being paranoid. What it does warrant is accepting the fact that we live in a violent world and should be prepared to deal with it. Remember, being prepared is not the same as being paranoid.

Our goal, therefore, is to have you consciously develop a feeling for how much risk you, as an individual, face in *your* circumstances, and decide how much effort you might *reasonably* wish to put into taking precautions to avoid problems. Think of reasonable in the context of driving: If you fasten your seatbelt, you have taken a reasonable precaution and greatly reduced your chance of injury in an accident. Reasonable precautions don't require you to lock yourself in a tower and isolate yourself from the world. That would be unreasonable.

Here's the bottom line with Step 1: Don't adopt the attitude that "It will never happen to me," or say that "If it's going to happen then it's going to happen," or think "I just don't have enough time to take precautions." Understand, accept, and deal with the reality and the risk of *your* being violently assaulted in your unique circumstances.

Other Risks

Before you worry about the dangers of violence, however, it is important that you consider other, greater health risks which you accept voluntarily. For example:

- If you smoke you are voluntarily taking an unnecessary risk.

- If you drink more than you should you are voluntarily taking an unnecessary risk.

- If you drink and drive you are voluntarily taking an unnecessary risk.

- If you don't take preventive care of your health you are voluntarily taking an unnecessary risk.

- If your diet is built around red meat and you never eat your veggies you are voluntarily taking an unnecessary risk.

- If you drive without wearing a seatbelt you are voluntarily taking an unnecessary risk.

- If you take drugs you are voluntarily taking an unnecessary risk.

- If you buy or sell drugs, or if you engage in other activities where you deal with violent people, you are voluntarily taking an unnecessary risk.

- If you are sexually active and do not practice safe sex every time you are voluntarily taking an unnecessary risk.

If you engage in these, or any other high-risk activities, we believe they should also be addressed at the same time as you concern yourself with your personal safety.

MENTALLY COMMIT TO DOING
EVERYTHING YOU CAN TO STAY SAFE

STEP 2
MENTALLY COMMIT TO DOING
EVERYTHING YOU CAN TO STAY SAFE

What Should You Do If Attacked?

The first question you should ask yourself is whether you should fight back if attacked, or if you should just plan on giving in. Obviously there is no one right answer that covers all situations. But statistics[3] do indicate that in a robbery you face a 75.3% chance of remaining unharmed if you are unarmed and submit, and that in a violent assault you face a 72.7% chance of remaining unharmed if you are unarmed and submit.

So what do these figures mean you should you do if, in spite of your best efforts, you are still the unlucky subject of violence? Should you submit or fight back? This is a tough decision, and your response should depend on the particular circumstances of the situation, your degree of preparation, and your best educated guess at the time.

It is our belief that if you do fight back, *proper training* will increase your chance of remaining

---

3. We will be quoting statistics throughout this book from Gary Kleck *Point Blank: Guns and Violence in America* (New York: Aldine de Gruyter, 1991).

unharmed, as well as increasing your chances of remaining unraped, unrobbed, and unmurdered.

In addition to helping you be prepared, training helps you to develop the mental commitment and *winning attitude* that is the critical factor in surviving a violent confrontation. It is your *winning attitude* that allows you to fight back at the appropriate time. It is your *winning attitude* that allows you to fight back effectively. It is your *winning attitude* that allows you to prevail—or at least survive—against an attacker capable of defeating you. And it is your *winning attitude* that allows you to come away from a violent confrontation feeling good about yourself and what you did, independent of the physical outcome.

On the down side, it is important to recognize that predators consider you their natural prey or crop, and deeply resent your challenging their God-given right to harvest you. If a predator has decided to attack you, it is because he or she has made the decision, as a risk-aversive businessperson, that you are an easy target. According to many police and corrections officers with whom we have spoken, prison interviews indicate that the two things that most frighten muggers and rapists are dogs (they cannot reason with or intimidate dogs) and people with guns who give the impression that they might use them. There is no safe middle ground between submission and shooting your assailant, and, as we will see, neither of these alternatives is totally safe, either.

The Four Priorities of Survival

When dealing with an actual confrontation that cannot be avoided, your primary goal is survival. The four priorities for surviving, in order of importance, are:

1. *Mental preparedness*: You are more likely to be able to avoid a confrontation if you're alert and prepared. If you are mentally prepared you will be able to deal with an unavoidable confrontation: You will be able either to avoid the confrontation, end the confrontation, or to survive it and still feel good about yourself. Thus mental preparedness is your top priority.
2. *Tactics*: Good tactics, in combination with mental preparedness, will help you deescalate a confrontation, and failing that, to get away, and failing that, to survive.
3. *Skill with your safety equipment*: Even if your tactics are good, if you are in a confrontation and rely on emergency safety tools—but can't make them work—you might as well not have them. Therefore it is important to have a good working knowledge of any equipment you choose to carry. Training and preparation are critical, since the outcome of an encounter will usually be decided in the first 5 to 10 seconds.

4. *Selection of optimum safety equipment*: This refers to choosing the most appropriate emergency safety tool. The equipment you choose is less important than your ability to use it, since any emergency safety tool used well is generally better than a more powerful emergency safety tool used poorly.

"The Decision"

We hope that by now you have consciously resolved to be *able* to defend yourself if appropriate, as well as to avoid trouble whenever possible. If so, you must make *The Decision*. The Decision is that you consciously vow that your life is worth fighting for, that you have a *right* and a *moral obligation* to defend yourself, and that you are *willing* do whatever is necessary to survive a violent confrontation, whether this means submitting if it is appropriate, or harming your assailant if it is necessary.

If you do make The Decision, commit mentally and physically to being a survivor. Make a firm resolution to do everything *within reason* to prepare for an assault. If you have never had any contact with violence, this will seem excessive and frightening. But if you plan for it and it someday happens, you will have the mindset for dealing with it and, more important, for surviving it. If it doesn't happen, it may be because you were prepared, so you lose nothing and may gain in terms of both personal safety and confidence.

Part of making The Decision is resolving that there is a line that you won't cross, an action you won't take. *Where* this line is drawn should be based on your realistic fear of being controlled by a person who wishes to do you harm. It means that you are willing to do whatever it takes to stay safe. It means that you may have to harm another person in order to prevent him or her from harming you or someone you love. Thus, for example, you may be willing to run away if someone snatches your gold chain, but if your child is at risk, or if someone tries to take you to an isolated area, you may may be willing to do your attacker great harm.

Even if you can't make The Decision, and decide to concentrate on risk-avoidance (which is where most of your effort should go in any case), we would still urge you to learn the physical skills involved in self-defense, as some feel strongly that to make a moral decision not to use force, the potential use of force must be an available option. And, of course, it would be nice to have the skills available if you change your mind later.

It is critical that everyone, both man and woman, come to an understanding of their feelings in this area *before* a confrontation occurs, since a timid effort at resistance can lead to the angry attacker hurting you as punishment for resisting.

Reducing Violence

Some say that there are two kinds of violent people: those violent by nature and those violent by nurture. There is little we can do in advance about those who are violent by nature. But we personally believe—albeit with no hard data to back us up[4]—that there is a lot we can do about those who will become violent because of poverty or social conditions. Since 70% of all violent crimes—mostly drug related—are committed by 6% of the violent criminals, every person who is kept out of this group makes a significant difference.

Therefore, while not directly related to the short-term issue of personal safety, we believe it is important that we all make a social commitment to dealing with those issues that foster violence. Unless we, as a society, commit to this, there is little chance that violence will be reduced.

There are three fundamental parts to this commitment. The first is assuring that all members of society are equipped to participate in society in a meaningful way. An underlying component of this is education. Education is the dividing line between the haves and the have-nots. If we do not work toward having a population with common values that can speak, read, reason, and manipu-

---

4. Dr. Arthur Kellerman of Emory University pointed out in congressional testimony that only $20,000,000 was spent on research on violence in 1989.

late numbers in a meaningful fashion, allowing gainful employment, we are condemned to a continuing cycle of poverty, crime, and violence. Sadly, a 1993 study by the United States Department of Education indicated that almost half of all Americans were, in effect, functionally illiterate.

In the same vein we must eliminate the predisposition toward violence that children develop when growing up with domestic violence. This transfer of violence from the home to the community does not help anyone fit in with society. According to congressional testimony by Dr. Beverly Jackson of the National Center for Clinical Infant Programs, domestic violence can be a significant factor in the creation of social violence.

The second part is assuring that members of society capable of participation are given the opportunity to participate. We must each, by our own speech and actions, and by our participation in community activities, work to break the cycle of hate, prejudice, and rage that infects our society, and to assure that merit is rewarded with advancement, independent of sex, race, or creed. This means not only avoiding bias ourselves, but also speaking out against prejudice and injustice when we come across it, rather than passively ignoring it, which is actually a tacit form of acceptance.

The third part is reducing glorification of violence in the media, and doing away with the view that violence is an acceptable problem-solving tool and acceptable behavior. While the media do not cause violent behavior, television, movies, and videos do an excellent job of both teaching new behavior and showing us that specific behaviors are legitimate and appropriate. And in movies and TV, violence is presented as the most effective—and in many cases the only—problem-solving tool. And in pornography, our largest selling class of video, violence toward women is presented as being acceptable behavior.

Perhaps worse, violence is offered as a tool that is free of consequences: On the screen you can stab, strike, sexually assault, or shoot someone and they either die cleanly or are back to normal by the end of the episode. What is never shown is the lifetime of disability and dysfunction, or the million-dollar health-care bills.

Children see hate and violence presented day after day, about once every six minutes on television as a whole. With this much institutionalized media violence working to desensitize them, there should be little surprise that there is so much youth violence, which then becomes institutionalized as adult violence.

How do we deal with this last piece of the puzzle? By voting with your dollars against violence: As an example, one of the authors of this book will not pay to see any movie with a gun in its advertisement. If more of us do this, maybe violence as entertainment will be reduced.

20

BE AWARE OF YOUR ENVIRONMENT
AND TAKE REASONABLE PRECAUTIONS

STEP 3
BE AWARE OF YOUR ENVIRONMENT
AND TAKE REASONABLE PRECAUTIONS

Violent Behavior

Before we get down to concrete preventive measures for reducing your risk from assault, you need a basic understanding of violent behavior.

Four Elements of Violent Behavior

Background or History

The first element of violent behavior is the *background or history* of the individual.

There is nothing you can do about a person's upbringing and background, but there are ways you can deal with people you know have a violent, irrational past, or strangers who give you reason to believe that they have a violent, irrational past. If a person has a history of violence and has a track record of irrational behavior, or is exhibiting one or more of the behavioral signs and cues we will list below, you should consider having nothing to do with him unless there are other, rational, people with you.

If you are alone with someone like this, you must anticipate potential danger. Even if they are a spouse, a parent, a sibling, a relative, a friend, a date, or a new acquaintance, you may have to run away for your own safety—even if it means running naked and screaming from your own home.

Reinforcement

The second element of violent behavior is the *reinforcement* available from the violent act.

In many cases you can't prevent the positive reinforcement that an attacker will get from assaulting you. There are, however, two things you can do: Try not to precipitate an assault by arguing with an emotional person (remember, the reward for assaulting you is shutting you up); conceal jewelry and other valuable items that might attract a mugger or robber, and minimize the amount of money you carry with you.

Opportunity and Risk

The third and fourth elements of violent behavior are the *opportunity* to commit an assault and the assailant's *risk* in the commission of the attack. These two go hand in hand and are factors over which you can have a degree of control.

If you eliminate the opportunity for someone to attack you then you can't be attacked. You haven't affected your attacker's desire to attack you, just his opportunity. Since it is easier to stay out of trouble than to get out of trouble, the ideal situation is to avoid confrontation.

Anticipating Violence

As part of growing up we gain knowledge and experience, and we predict and anticipate things based on what we have learned. When it comes to dealing with a person who might become violent, we can learn to recognize those circumstances, behaviors, and bodily cues that may come before an assault.

Circumstances That Lead to Violence

Social Interaction

Both parties in most murder[5] and rape[6] cases are members of the same social class and residential area. Murders, assaults, and rapes are usually committed by friends, relatives, and associates. They often occur in private, without a prior break-in or illegal entry. Where the assailant knows the

---

5. In the case of murder by an acquaintance, the average person murdered is a career criminal killed by a disgruntled confederate or a spouse killed at the end of a long history of physical violence. This means that if you are not now involved in violence, you face a reduced probability of being murdered. The exception to this, according to the January 1993 Bureau of Justice Statistics National Update, is that if you are over age 65 you are more likely to be killed by a stranger during the commission of a felony. But even then, while those older than 65 comprise about 14% of the sample population, they are involved in less than 2% of all violent incidents.

6. As an example, according to Donna Chaiet of prePARE, Inc., in New York City, over 50% of all rapes are categorized as acquaintance/date rapes.

person being assaulted, the person is usually assaulted inside a house or an apartment or some other private area, then dragged somewhere even more private.

Such assaults almost always involve arguments or social interactions, and the person being assaulted often inadvertently precipitates the act through criminal activity, insults, drinking, or sexual overtures. These assaults are, in most cases, a response aimed at ending a punishing stimulus, or a stimulus that somehow reinforces behavior that is negative rather than positive. They are *not* the fault of the person being assaulted.

Risk for the Assailant

Most violence that occurs outside the home is usually committed by the sociopathic predator. A sociopath is a person whose behavior is largely amoral and asocial, and who is characterized by irresponsibility, a lack of remorse, shame, or sense of wrongdoing, and perverse and impulsive behavior. The problem with attackers of this type is that not only are they opportunists, but they are also professionals in the sense that they have plans and strategies for committing their crimes. Getting caught, injured, or killed is a calculated risk they have already factored in, with the potential gain balanced against the risk of punishment. Unfortunately, the risk factor from our current criminal justice system is low in most cases. It is estimated that for every 100 serious crimes only 5 criminals go to jail. And the average time served on a life sentence is 7.75 years.

Danger Zones

Danger zones are distances between people and things that jeopardize our personal safety.

We classify distances for normal American[7] social interaction as follows:

Public: 12 or more feet away.
Social: 4 to 12 feet away.
Personal: 2 to 4 feet away.
Intimate: direct contact to 2 feet away.

We all lead busy lives in which we are constantly moving between work, restaurants, the theater, sporting events, and home. We travel on foot and on public transport with people we don't know. We have learned that in certain situations— waiting in line, riding a full elevator, or taking in a ball game—it is reasonable to be shoulder-to-shoulder with total strangers.

---

7. In other cultures these distances are different from ours. Thus, a European is likely to consider Americans cold because we want to carry on a social conversation at 4 to 12 feet, where they are most comfortable at 2 to 4 feet. Americans may consider Europeans "sexy" because they make social or personal contacts at distances which are, by American standards, personal or intimate.

Anytime people are within these distances, whether you know them or not, the distance should be appropriate for the situation. If not, you should deal with them on your own terms, or at least in terms that are appropriate for the situation.

We have also learned that in situations where we're not forced together by public congestion, it is not reasonable for people to get too close to us.

Anytime we're with people we don't know, it is a warning sign when someone is closing in on us, unless we've initiated it. If you are walking down the street or walking toward your parked car and someone starts moving toward you, you need to be on guard.

Attackers seldom tip their hand until they can get close enough to grab you without having to risk chasing you. They will try to stay as nonthreatening as possible until they think they are close enough to surprise you. Strangers may call for you to stop or "wait a minute." They may ask for you to come over and help them or they may offer to help you, even when you don't need any help.

Someone standing in a dark or shadowed area, behind trees, parked cars, the corner of a building, in a stairway, etc., is indicating unreasonable— and therefore suspicious—behavior. In this situation it is wise to make brief eye contact, so they know that you are aware of them, but not steady eye contact, which may be taken as a challenge.

When women are attacked, it is common for assailants to stalk them, attacking from behind. So stay alert!

If what is happening seems unreasonable to you, you may feel that you are in danger. If you feel that you are in danger of being assaulted then you need to be aware of the distances at which you are vulnerable to specific attacks. If the attacker:

- Is unarmed: If he is within 10 feet, you are in danger of not being able to get safely away.

- Has an edged weapon or club: If he is within 21 feet, and there isn't a solid barrier between the two of you, then you are in danger of not being able to get away, and not having sufficient time to defend yourself.

- Has a gun: If he can see you, and there is nothing between the two of you that will stop bullets, then he can shoot you.

In most cases, however, an attacker is going to get as close to you as he can before the assault.

The most important thing to understand is how fast someone can get to you from distances that may seem safe to you, and that you believe—falsely—will give you enough time to act and respond. The average attacker can cover 5 feet in under a quarter of a second, 10 feet in under three-quarters of a second, and 21 feet in under one and a half seconds. A second and a half isn't a lot of time. In fact, it's less time than it takes most of us just to recognize that something is happening, whether or not we are expecting trouble.

And it's not just you. In training police officers it becomes clear that at 21 feet or closer it's unlikely that an officer under attack can draw his or her weapon and fire. Check this for yourself by performing a Tuller Drill, named for Dennis Tuller of Salt Lake City: Have a friend stand 21 feet away from you and see how long it takes for him or her to run up to you and pretend to stab you.

Awareness

The most important factor in avoiding confrontation is awareness. You must be aware of your environment. The military has long color-coded levels of awareness in order to make them easier to conceptualize.

The worst state of awareness you can be in is *Condition White*: You are totally unaware of your surroundings and totally unprepared for even the prospect of danger. This state is the reason that so many muggings take place between 4 and 6 p.m., when people are just getting off work and are in a fog. Condition White seems to attract predators, who are able to recognize this vulnerable state.

In *Condition Yellow* you are relaxed but alert. You are not expecting trouble, but you are aware of your environment, so you would recognize a problem if it arose. This should be your normal state; merely being in Condition Yellow should allow you to avoid those few violent confrontations you might otherwise face in your lifetime.[8]

In addition to making you aware of potential problems, awareness of your environment makes you equally aware of the good things happening around you. This is important for a full life.

Condition Orange is a state of general alarm: You are aware that there seems to be a problem and your body is reacting. You are trying to analyze and avoid the problem, and possible defensive tactics are being considered.

In *Condition Red* the problem has occurred, and you are facing one or more opponents you reasonably believe might do you harm. You should be taking cover and actively performing the appropriate defensive tactics. If already under attack, you are working to neutralize the threat.

Condition Black is a state of blind panic, where you are unable to react to the situation because you have developed neither the inner tools nor the outer skills with which to react.

Awareness, however, is of little value unless you know what to be aware of.

---

8. One serial killer, Ted Bundy, reputedly said that his initial selection was based on whether his potential victims were alert and aware of their environment. If they were alert and aware of what was going on around them, then he would look for someone else.

The Etheric Experience, Behavioral Warning Signs, and Pre-attack Cues

Our bodies and their reactions have not changed since cave dwellers first fought or ran from wild animals. Back then, thousands of years ago, the body went through both psychological and physiological changes when its owner was threatened. This is known as the *fight-or-flight* response.

Even today, at the end of the 20th century, when we feel we are in danger of being hurt emotionally or physically, or are anxious about something, we go through the same changes in our emotional and physical behaviors that our primitive forebears went through eons ago. And we all learn to tell— often without knowing how—that other people are upset, angry, frustrated, depressed, anxious, afraid, violent, or aggressive. We can categorize the clues that allow us to "read" other people as *etheric experience*, *behavioral warning signs*, and *pre-attack cues*.

Etheric Experience

It is not yet clear exactly what the etheric experience actually is, but for practical purposes it may be thought of as the feeling that something is wrong. While a great deal of scientific effort is being devoted to understanding the physical characteristics of the etheric experience, especially by the Russians, from our point of view if it *feels* as though something is wrong or as if some bad thing is about to happen, assume that something is wrong or that some bad thing is about to happen, and take appropriate action.

Women tend to be more willing to act on these feelings than men. In general, men wait until there is some physical manifestation to evaluate, and often end up having to deal with a problem that might have been avoided. Women police officers start out being sensitive to these feelings but often end up badly influenced by their male counterparts, learn to surpress these feelings, and so get injured needlessly. Again, if it *feels* wrong, assume that it is wrong.

Behavioral Warning Signs

If someone you know gets violent when they get upset or drunk, you should put distance between the two of you when they drink or get upset. Just leave when they get this way, even if it means running away from your own home.

But even strangers can give valuable clues as to their state of mind and intentions, which can give you time to prepare or flee. These clues include:

- Increasing level of agitation: This indicates that the individual is becoming more irrational, aggressive, and volatile.

- Excessive emotional attention toward you: This indicates that you are their primary focus.

- Conspicuously ignores you: This indicates they might be setting you you up for a sucker punch.

- Exaggerated movements (such as pacing back and forth, finger pointing, belligerent verbal dialogue): These indicate that this individual is losing rational control.

- Facial color changes to flushed: This indicates that there is a great change in the body's internal and emotional functioning. (A flushed face may be the body's primitive way of making itself look scarier.)

- Ceasing all movement: If the individual goes from moving and talking with anxious intensity to stopping all movement and talking, it may be the "calm before the storm."

- Changes from total lack of cooperation to total cooperation: This may indicate you are being set up for an attack.

Pre-Attack Cues

Pre-attack cues are even clearer signs of imminent danger. Some of these are:

- Shifting one foot in back of the other, often to a boxer's stance, so the body is more stable, and can move toward you more easily.

- Clenching the fists, to prepare for attack by "lubricating" the finger joints, and to keep under control.

- Shifting the shoulders back, a primitive body sign designed to give you the message that they mean business, as well as providing a certain amount of protection, or as preparation for striking you.

- Looking for a weapon to attack with or at a specific area on your body. (This may be a *target glance*.)

- Conspicuously looking elsewhere while talking with you. (They may be trying to distract you prior to a surprise attack, or checking out their post-attack escape route.)

- Depersonalizing you, which may show as a *thousand-yard stare*. (A good example of this can be seen in the movie *The Silence of the Lambs*, when Anthony Hopkins looks at Jody Foster as if she weren't even there.) The subject might be depersonalizing you so that they are attacking a thing rather than a person.

- Hiding or averting the face. (Sometimes people who are on the verge of losing control of themselves perform a *facial wipe*, by which they attempt to hide the level of anxiety they're experiencing by physically moving their hands over their faces. This may show up as removing a hat, slicking back the hair, or something equally innocuous.)

- Bobbing up and down or rocking back and forth on the balls of the feet. (As people get more upset, these movements act as a means of diffusing the adrenalin and anxiety.)

- Growling. (At the peak of their fear or anger, some people growl before they attack.)

- Lowering the body slightly, causing the head to lower, just before moving in for the attack. (This can be quite significant, as it is very difficult to move forward without a prior downward shift of body weight. Indeed, even cars sink somewhat before accelerating.)

- Facial coloring changing from flushed to pale. (The body is moving blood from the extremities to the internal organs, to protect them in case of injury.)

Be aware of and look for these feelings, behaviors, and cues, as they are clear signs of danger. When you see these signs, you should try to calm this person down, to create safe distance between you, or to place a solid object between you.

Safety Tips

Most predators don't like people seeing what they're doing, because it makes them conspicuous, easier to avoid, and more easily identified. So you should function in a way that puts would-be attackers at risk of being seen and then caught.

Places that are poorly lit and offer hiding places, such as parks at night, walkways, empty streets, parking garages, and lots provide an opportunity for a "crime against a person."

Many apartment complexes, condominiums, even private homes have been designed to look inward on themselves, so that residents don't have to look at the bordering streets. As a result, these streets have been deprived of natural surveillance by residents, and often turn out to be unsafe for both residents and members of the surrounding community. Many people now stay at home rather than risk going out at night, making neighborhoods emptier and adding to feelings of insecurity.

Areas that have both residential and commercial use 24 hours a day are safer. Streets that have pedestrian and vehicular traffic, small shops and cafés open late at night, and residents living in apartments or houses overlooking the street are safer streets. Because they have multiple purposes, such streets "have eyes."

Areas with multiple uses—restaurants, theaters, zoos, movie houses, art galleries—are safer because they *are* more used, more populated, and, thus, have natural surveillance.

Natural surveillance creates an overall image of a safer environment, and significantly reduces the paranoia, fear, stress, and anxiety all of us feel when we are put into a questionable situation. It is more than image, however. It is also a deterrent against violence since this image becomes reality when the predator, who is more aware of the environment and the perception of risk than you are, chooses to go elsewhere.

The goal is to spend your time in places where there are lots of other people, all of whom are going about their business safely and prudently, just like you.

Circumstances don't always provide you with a highly public environment. In these cases:

General Tips

- Setting boundaries in nonthreatening social situations should be done reasonably but firmly, without confrontation and aggression which could escalate to violence. You need to *name the behavior* and *demand that it stop*. Although the examples given below are more likely to happen to women than to men, our desire here is to deal with boundary violations without escalating to aggression or violence, rather than offering dating advice.

  For example, if someone you know puts their arm around you, you can say—loudly if there are other people around—"I feel uncomfortable when you do that. Please take your arm away." This puts *you* in control of *your* feelings, and tells them what *you* want done.

  If the person tries to make this seem like your fault by saying something like "This didn't bother you before" or, in a sexual situation when dealing with a manipulative swine—whom you probably shouldn't be dating—"You would if you loved me," you can say "It's not alright now," or merely repeat "I feel uncomfortable when you do that. Take your arm away" as you physically remove their arm.

Note that initially saying "Please take your arm away" shows control with politeness, while saying "Take your arm away, please" has an imploring quality lacking control.

This technique works in a wide variety of situations, from annoying siblings or roommates who come into your bedroom without knocking, to maiden aunts pinching your cheeks at weddings.

Setting boundaries in nonthreatening public situations also requires naming the behavior and demanding that it stop.

For example, If you are on a crowded bus and some stranger puts his hand on you, you might grab the hand, lift it up, and say, loudly so everyone can hear "What is this hand doing on my body?"

In some cases inappropriate behavior can be dealt with even more subtly. Patricia Ireland, attorney, president of the National Organization of Woman (NOW), and dedicated feminist, tells of walking into a board room and being told by some man to fetch a cup of coffee. Her response was to get the coffee, bring it to him, and then take her place at the head of the table next to the CEO as corporate counsel. The behavior was never repeated.

- Be definite about your limits and decide before-hand where you will draw the line. Make it clear that you mean what you say. If the individual does not comply with what you say, then it's time to get up and get away, even if it means leaving your own home.

- If you are assaulted, your assailant may try to convince you to go with him to some other place, promising that you won't be hurt if you comply. Or if you're near your car, he might want to get into the car with you. In general, assailants want to take you from a place that's too public for them to a place that's too private for you.

  Current wisdom says that going to a more private place significantly increases your level of risk, and, therefore, is crossing the line. Since if you leave with them you're likely to be hurt anyway, this is probably a good time to start fighting back.

- It is very important to trust your gut feelings. If you feel that somehow things just don't seem right, they probably aren't, so get out of there!

- Try to avoid following set patterns: Don't leave your home the same time every day, or travel the same route every day, or come home the same way at the same time every day. This unpredictability may induce a predator to go after someone with a more predictable lifestyle.

- While not within the scope of this book, in domestic violence—spousal or child abuse— cognitive dissonance theory practically forces you to say "I must really love my spouse/parent because I am putting up with this, and therefore, while horrible, I should stay because [fill in a seemingly valid reason here]." It is also difficult to leave if you have nowhere to go or are a child. But domestic violence is never justified, and domestic violence is one of the major causes of injury to women: Please try to get someone to help you break this cycle. If you have been isolated from friends and family, your local social services agency, or the police, or the National Coalition Against Domestic Violence (located in Colorado) can help get you moving in a safer direction.

- Whenever reasonable, let someone else know where you are and what time you should be somewhere else. Maybe have someone call you, or you call them. This type of procedure will provide a very tactful message to an individual who is unexpectedly putting you at risk. If you're at a party, for example, and someone asks you to go somewhere, tell other people where you're going and with whom. If you later end up in a bad situation, you can always remind this person that several people know you left together.

- Avoid traveling alone, particularly at night.

- Develop and practice verbalization skills. Say things to the individual that mean exactly what you say and say exactly what you mean. We will discuss this further in Step 4 in the "Physical Skills for Self-Defense" section under "Verbal Stunning."

- Be aware that Westley Allan Dodd, a serial rapist/killer who preyed on prepubescent boys, said in public interviews that at least four of his potential victims, in the 4- to 6-year-old range, remained unmolested and alive because their parents had taught them to run away, yelling, from bad people.

- If you are a woman, try not to go out with men who are disrespectful of women, or whose lives are based around breaking rules.

- Since 70% of all violent crimes are committed by 6% of all violent criminals (of which a goodly portion are drug related) you should not involve yourself with criminal activities, or with drugs, or with anything else that puts you in contact with criminals.

- When teaching children about not dealing with strangers, remember that, from a child's point of view, any adult with whom they have spoken for even a few minutes is not a stranger.

In Your Car

- Park in well-lit areas. Don't frequent stores where there's no safe parking.

- Frequent stores that offer a carry-out service.

- Don't hinder movements by carrying packages in your arms. Use a push cart instead.

- Be cautious if there's a van with sliding doors parked next to your car in an isolated parking lot: You should get into your car from the side opposite the van.

- Before getting in your car, look to make sure that no one is hiding in it, *including the back seat.* If possible, check that no one is hiding under it as you approach. Immediately lock the doors once you get in.

- Keep your car doors locked at all times, and the windows up as much as possible.

- Reduce the risk of a smash-and-rob by keeping packages on the floor, not on the front seat.

- Keep your car in good repair and full of gas.

- Don't pick up hitchhikers for any reason.

- Leave enough space in front of you when stopped so that you can escape by driving around the car in front in case of trouble.

- Drive to a safe place before changing a flat.

- If you suspect you're being followed by another car, make a few turns randomly to make sure. Don't stop and don't get out of your car. Use your horn and lights, and your ability to keep driving, to try to attract attention. Look for help—a police car or police station. If possible, see what make, model, and color the car is, and get the license number if you can.

- If someone bumps into your car in an isolated area, don't get out of the car to discuss the incident, as they may be robbers or carjackers setting you up. Instead, tell them to follow you, while you drive, flashers flashing, to a place where there are a lot of people around.

- If stopped by a plainclothes policeman in an unmarked car in an isolated area, be very suspicious, since one television report indicated that there were roughly 25,000 crimes committed by fake cops each year. It is better to drive to an area where there are people around, then deal with the problem.

- Carry a cellular phone with you so you can call the police from your car in case of trouble.

At Home

- The best burglar alarm you can have is a dog.

- If you have an answering machine, don't leave messages with your name saying that you aren't home or indicating that you live alone. Instead, say something on the order of "We can't come to the phone right now, but if you'll leave a message after the tone signal, we'll get back to you as soon as possible." This gives the impression may or may not be home, and that if you are home you aren't home alone.

- Don't put your name on your mail box.

- Don't discard mail with your name and address on it in public trash cans.

- If you come home and the door is open, or if you suspect that someone has been in your home, *don't go in* to check. Instead, call the police and let them check. You may feel foolish if no one is there or if your kid brother has come to visit, but feeling foolish is better than being attacked by a prowler.

- Have dead bolts on all exterior doors.

- Place secondary locks on all windows and interior doors. Check to make sure your children haven't left them open at night.

- Don't open your door to everyone who rings your doorbell. Look through the peephole, then open the door. Have children do the same.

- When you answer the phone or door, don't tell the caller that you live or are alone. Instead, say that you don't want to disturb your resting companion, spouse, parent, or whatever.

- Don't let a stranger into your home. If someone attempts to get you to let him use your phone, offer to call for them if you believe his request is legitimate. If not, call the police. Don't be afraid or embarrassed to call for assistance if you might need it, and don't be embarrassed to say you don't let strangers in.

- If someone breaks in at night, lock the bedroom door, call the police (perhaps on your cellular phone so you can't be cut off), and toss them your keys when they arrive.

- Leave lights on in different areas to confuse a potential attacker about your location.

- If you light the outside of your home, have lights aimed toward the house. This allows neighbors as well as the police to see people trying to enter.

On the Street

- If you're walking from one location to another, go out of your way to travel in areas that are well lit and provide you with high surveillance opportunities.

- Walk near the street side of a sidewalk (but not too near), rather than the building side. In case of problems you can run into the street, and it's harder to drag you into a doorway.

- When going around a corner, go around it as widely as possible. If you cut too close to the corner, and there is someone lurking on the other side, you will walk right into them. It is better to have enough space to allow yourself to react.

- In some environments a personal alarm, which makes a very loud noise, can help create unnatural surveillance where no natural surveillance exists.

- If you're leaving a building such as a theater, museum, or mall, and you feel that you may be in danger, go back into the building and try another exit, or get someone such as a security officer to walk with you or to get you a ride.

- Avoid shortcuts through vacant lots, deserted parks, empty parking garages and unlit areas, especially at night.

- Consider carrying a pocket-sized high-intensity flashlight. If there are dark or shadowed areas, illuminate them so that you can see.

- If accosted, consider tossing money in one direction while you run, yelling, in another. It is very important that you begin moving away from your attacker as soon as you throw the money, as often these people will grab the money and either hit you in the face or slash you with a knife so that you will be distracted, terrified, upset, and not remember what they looked like. It may be worth carrying a few dollars separately, just to throw.

- If you're walking, jogging, or running and someone is stalking you in a car, consider running back the way you came—it may be hard for them to turn around or back up.

- Be aware that if you are in public wearing headphones, you may not hear anything going on around you and may become significantly less aware of your environment.

- If possible, don't put keys, money, credit cards, or anything else you don't want to lose in a knapsack, bag, or purse which can be snatched.

- Remember, if you stop and turn aggressively toward someone who turns out to be an innocent citizen "doing his thing," you don't care if he thinks you're crazy. At least you're safe and didn't take an unnecessary risk. Whenever in doubt, take the necessary precautions.

- Don't carry anything you don't absolutely need on any trip.

- When using a pay telephone on the street, turn around and face outward after dialing.

- Purse snatchers—who grab bags from men as well as women—tend to be violent if thwarted. It might therefore make sense to let your bag go rather than get into a fight.

In Public Places

- Don't assume that the operators of a public place have taken adequate security precautions. They haven't!

- Check out the layout of the facility you are in. Look for your escape route.

- If you work in a store, don't put both your first and last name on your name badge.

- Don't put ID down on a counter where other people can read your name and address.

- Don't sit near the cash register in bars and restaurants, as these are the most likely places for robberies. Instead, sit near a service exit if possible. This will allow you to make a break for the kitchen, and then out the back door, in case of an emergency.

- Don't get into an elevator if you feel uncomfortable about the people already in, or getting in, with you. Don't worry about hurting their feelings—just don't get in. One woman of our acquaintance won't get into an elevator alone with any man she doesn't know.

- In hotels, which have become more dangerous over the past few years, be sure to use the chain lock on your door: While hotels are supposed to change the lock when a key is missing, they frequently don't.

- Don't let anyone you don't know into your hotel room. If you receive a call saying that there's a problem in the room and that a repairman is coming up, call the front desk to make sure there really is a repairman coming; the "repairman" could turn out to be a robber.

- If there's no major price difference between a single room and a double, it's worth taking the room as a double, saying that your companion will be arriving shortly. This will tell an "inside" person that he and his accomplices should look elsewhere for a single occupancy. And if you get a call asking if the room is single or double occupancy, always say that it's a double with two people.

- Most hotels offer safety deposit boxes. If you are obvious about putting valuables which are not immediately needed into the safety deposit box, this tells inside robbers that it is not worth breaking into your room while you are there. Or, for that matter, while you aren't there.

- In a public men's room, use a stall rather than a urinal: Standing preoccupied at a urinal with your back to the world you are very vulnerable.

- Before leaving a bathroom stall, check under the door to see if there are any feet lurking there.

- If some crazy person starts shooting a gun anywhere near you, whether during a robbery, a drive-by shooting, an assault, or for some totally unknown reason, immediately drop to the floor or ground, keep as low as possible, and crawl to safety if possible, or under something or behind something.

GET AWAY BY CREATING
AND MAINTAINING DISTANCE

STEP 4
GET AWAY BY CREATING
AND MAINTAINING DISTANCE

Attempting to get away from your assailant has two virtues. First, you will hopefully get to safety. The second, and more important, virtue is that it creates distance and puts you in a better position from which to defend yourself if you can't get away. However, this is not totally free from risk: Gary Kleck indicates that nonviolent resistance, including evasion, gives you a 65.1% chance of remaining unharmed in a robbery and a 74.5% chance of remaining unharmed in an assault. This rate is worse for you in a robbery, and essentially the same in an assault. What this means is that even if you choose to run away you may still have to deal with the assault.

Success Factors in Self-Defense

Having made the decision to take positive steps to ensure your personal safety, you now need to take a look at those factors and techniques that will help keep you safe, as well as the physical skills necessary to make these techniques work. Understand that techniques don't exist in isolation. You must think of how each of them would apply in real life.

You must ask yourself how they would apply if you were having an argument that turned violent, if you opened the door and someone pushed his way in, if you were walking down the street and someone followed you or confronted you for money, or if you were at work or on a date and your partner forced sexual attentions on you.

Once it's clear that you can't avoid a confrontation, the most important thing to do is to immediately implement your self-defense plans—which we will begin developing in this step—rather than hesitate and react unproductively. There are four factors that influence the success of these plans.

Reflexive Response

When you are attacked, your *fight-or-flight* mechanism kicks in, preparing you to either fight and stay safe or run to safety. It is estimated that over 144 psycho-physiological and 1,400 psycho-chemical reactions take place simultaneously during this period of intense stress. One of the most critical reactions is that your brain gives over conscious thought to reflex action, *assuming that you have training on which you can fall back reflexively.* Anything less than a reflexive response by you in an attack situation will cause you to think consciously—and conscious thought takes time you just don't have. If you have no training on which to fall back, then you're likely to fall into the blind panic of Condition Black.

The best way to successfully stop an assault is to respond reflexively. This is because if you're being attacked you have to *either* recognize that you're under attack (which takes time) and reflexively react *or* recognize that you are being attacked (which takes time), decide how to respond, and then respond—which takes too long if you need conscious thought. When you counterattack, your attacker in turn has to overcome the time lag required to identify and react to your counterattack. Remember, your attacker is counting on surprising you, with no anticipation that you will fight back. When you counterattack it's unexpected and disconcerting to your attacker, and with some luck you will catch him off guard.

Intensity

Defensive action should be an all-or-nothing response. You are more likely to perform at 100% output capacity if your response is reflexive. That means reflexively running as fast as you can, reflexively striking as hard as you can, or reflexively yelling a command as loudly as you can.

Technique

To make any technique work you need to be able to do three things: First, you need to be able, under stress, to reflexively choose an appropriate technique. It's also a good idea to know the specific name of the technique you employ. This is important for your legal survival if you're taken to court for defending yourself: Being able to cite the name of the technique you utilized will add credibility to the fact that you were trained and competent.

Second, you need to be able to reflexively perform the technique under stress. Be aware that in a dynamic situation you may have to reflexively change techniques as the situation changes.

Finally, you need to know what the technique is supposed to do. This allows you to know if it is working, and gives you a self-fulfilling expectation for your technique.

Practice

The only way to achieve reflex action and do a technique properly under stress is to establish and excite an appropriate neural pathway in that part of your brain where reflex action and physical movements are stored. It is estimated that it will take between 300 and 3,000 repetitions to achieve the beginnings of reflex action under stress, so you'll need to practice the techniques you learn in this book until you are comfortable with them.

We all know that practice makes perfect. What we sometimes forget is that it is only *perfect* practice that makes perfect. In order to successfully do a technique under stress, whatever practice you do must be as near-perfect as possible, since what you do under stress will be done *faster* and *worse* than what you do in practice.

Some of the practice must be physical repetitions. The rest can be a mixture of *visualization*, where you practice (perfectly) in your imagination, and *dream practice*, which tends to allow more realistic scenarios than does visualization. While it takes a bit of practice to learn to direct and control your dreams, stopping and replaying them, it's a skill well worth developing. We will deal with practice techniques again in Step 5.

Physical Skills for Self-Defense

In order to safely get away from an attacker you need to develop physical skills related to your personal safety. But before you practice these skills you need to prepare your body *and* your mind. This preparation is called a *tactical warm-up*, because the heating and stretching movements used are the same as used for defense. While you won't have time for this sort of preparation when attacked, a tactical warm-up is important before practicing to prevent injury during training, as well as to put you in the right frame of mind. And, after training, it's important to go through a *cool-down* period, where you do simple movements such as walking in place while swinging your arms lightly, while your blood pressure moves back to a normal range. While a warm-up is designed to protect your muscles, a cool-down allows your dilated blood vessels to contract to normal size.

Without a cool-down it is possible for the blood pressure to fall rapidly as your pulse decreases, causing fainting or worse—much worse! Like a heart attack!

A detailed tactical warm-up is in Appendix B.

Weapon Hand and Reaction Hand

Throughout this book we will be using the terms *weapon hand* and *reaction hand*. In general, the weapon hand is the hand in which you would hold a gun: the right hand if you're right-handed and the left hand if you're left-handed. The reaction hand is your other hand, and is used, as implied by the name, to react to the subject, to keep him at a distance, and for other supplementary tasks. The reaction foot, weapon foot, reaction side, and weapon side are, obviously, on the same sides of your body as the reaction or weapon hand.

Verbal Stunning

Speaking is also a physical skill, and under stressful conditions you want to say things that you have trained yourself to say. Practice saying and yelling such one- or two-word commands as:

No!
Stop!
Back!
Stop! Back!
Stay back!

Loud, repetitive verbal commands can often shock or stun your attacker, who is expecting nothing other than compliance from you. Verbal stunning is a *critical* part of your defensive actions: Techniques that may work perfectly in conjunction with verbal stunning may not work alone. Verbal stunning is so important we will discuss it further in Step 5 in the "Techniques and Tactics" section under "Verbal Stunning."

Stance: The Pyramid Base Foot Position and the Centering Concept

Proper stance gives you a look of confidence and assertiveness (which may help to avoid a conflict) and achieves a secure foot position from which it is easy to move to either escape or to defend yourself if necessary.

To find your correct stance you'll need to form a *pyramid base* with your feet, and then lower your *center*, keeping your head vertically over your hips. Your center is your body's center of gravity. A male's center is about three fingers below belly-button level, and a female's center is a little lower, about at pelvis level.

So when we say "Assume a pyramid base and center yourself," we mean:

1. Put your reaction foot forward and your weapon foot back.
2. Turn your weapon foot out 60 degrees.
3. Put a slight bend in your knees.

4. Place your body weight on the balls of your feet but keep your heels flat.
5. Keep your head directly over your hips. Avoid leaning forward, backward, or to the side because this unbalances you and makes it hard for you to regain your balance. (You can check your balance by bouncing lightly on your toes.)
6. Hold your hands up at least as high as your lower ribs. Keeping your hands down at your sides slows your response time because of the extra distance your hands have to travel.

The Benefits of a Pyramid Base

Besides giving you a more assertive image, there are other benefits of assuming a pyramid stationary base:

- Increased balance and improved response time: Having your feet wide and deep—still keeping your weight on the balls of your feet—will give you stability front, back, and side, while putting you in a stance from which you can move without readjusting your body.

- A smaller target is presented: By turning your rear foot out 60 degrees, your body turns too, and from the front you present a smaller target to an attacker.

- Vulnerable organs are protected: This stance protects such vital areas as your throat, solar-plexus, abdomen, and groin.

- Impact deflection: If the attacker is grabbing or striking at you, your angled body will deflect his energy away from you.

- Common stance: During an attack, you need to respond reflexively without conscious thought. By having one stance (even though it may have varying width and depth), you'll be able to both defend and escape without needing to worry about changing foot position.

Stationary Stances

When you're standing still, you should be in a pyramid base foot position and centered. Now, depending on your assessment of the threat being presented, you should increase the width and depth of your stance, which will lower your center. The wider and longer your pyramid base, the harder it will be to move you (and to move yourself), and the easier for you to defend yourself.

There are three variations in stationary stance:

Conversational Stance

In this stance you are standing inconspicuously in a small pyramid base with your feet placed slightly less than shoulder width apart and about the same amount deep, and with your body turned to your weapon side (i.e., with your reaction foot forward). Make this your normal everyday stance. In this stance you are prepared to act, but nobody else knows it.

Ready Stance

If you're in a situation where something doesn't feel right, or you see behavioral warning signs, it's time to anticipate potential danger and get ready to deal with it.

For the ready stance, simply increase the width and depth of your pyramid foot position by about an additional half foot over your conversational stance. Still keep your weight on the balls of your feet. Depending on what is happening, you may have immediately assumed a ready stance, by-passing the conversational stance.

Defensive Stance

Once you're actively in danger or actually being attacked, shift to the defensive stance. This is the stance to be in when you're physically keeping an attacker at bay. Increase the width and depth of your pyramid base as much as you comfortably can while still keeping your weight on the balls of your feet, thus retaining the ability to move. Bouncing lightly on the balls of your feet will help keep you centered and will provide a moving base from which to start running. It may also confuse your attacker.

As with the conversational and ready stances, you may have to immediately assume a defensive stance based on what's happening at the time, for example if you're walking to your car and are suddenly assaulted.

Patterns of Movement

The purpose of the pyramid base foot position is to help you to fend off an attacker or to get away from an attack. Obviously, this means that you're not going to stand still. If you are under attack, you should be thinking, "Feet do your stuff and get me outta here!!!"

Getting away involves going from standing still to running. Whether you're under attack and are actively defending yourself, or you're struggling to get away, or you've broken free and are running, you need to be able to move while still maintaining the stability of the pyramid base. So even if you can get away without having to actually fight with your attacker, your best bet to overcome the inertia of standing still is to start your escape from a pyramid base foot position. This is as true for a small woman in a dress as it is for a 200-pound male in pants.

You will go from your pyramid base to motion through use of *patterns of movement*. The rule of thumb for patterns of movement says that the foot closest to the direction you want to go takes the first step, and the other one follows.

Step-and-Drive Escape

Assume you are facing an attacker, and your escape route is straight behind you. If you're in a pyramid base with your reaction foot forward, you should just step back with your weapon foot and start running. When you take the first step with your weapon foot—the foot closest to the direction you want to run—you will naturally drive your body weight off your reaction foot as you escape. Avoid crossing your legs in front of you, where one leg steps over and across the other—crossed legs are very unstable, and can cause you to lose your balance and trip.

This *step-and-drive* pattern of movement is how you should move your feet as you get away and then run away from the attacker. Step-and-drive escaping is the pattern of movement you will use most often. However, there are times that, depending on the position or angle from which the assailant is coming toward you, you may need to use a different initial movement.

Pivoting and Stepping Through

If you are facing an attacker—again with your reaction foot forward—and your escape route is behind the attacker to your weapon side, you will have to run past him to get away. Slash at him with the closest hand to distract him if he is too close and start running. In this situation you will pivot on your forward reaction foot—the movement a smoker performs when he puts out a cigarette on the ground with the ball of his foot—as you step through with your weapon foot.

Obviously, if your escape route is in back of your attacker on the other side—your reaction side—you would do a step-and-drive escape past him starting with your reaction foot.

Sweep-and-Go

Sometimes an attacker may get so close to you that you need to create distance from him with some initial, but minimal, contact. If the attacker is close enough to grab at you, but not so close as to eliminate your ability to get away, you may be able to sweep his incoming hands away from you as you simultaneously run to your escape route. Here's how to do the *sweep-and-go*:

1. Get into your pyramid base stationary stance. The width and depth you choose—ready stance, conversational stance, or defensive stance—should match the spontaneousness and seriousness of the assault.
2. Bring both your hands up and sweep the incoming attacker's hands and arms *away from* the direction you want to escape to. This sweeping movement is a crescent arcing movement which forces the attacker's arms up and away from you. You may sweep to the right or to the left, depending on the direction you want to go in your escape. If you want to escape to your left, sweep the attacker's incoming arm to your right. If you want to escape to the right, sweep the attacker's arms to your left. As you sweep the incoming assault away from you, shout at the assailant "Stay back!"

3. Run to your escape route while you shout "Help! Help! Fire! Fire!" (Shouting "Fire!" is more likely to bring help because people need to confirm that *they* might be in danger, too.)
4. Keep running until you're safe.

Step-and-Drag Stepping

If the attacker grabs you, you have to keep from falling or being pushed to the ground.

If your attacker is pulling at you or pushing you, perhaps trying to drag you somewhere, you need to keep a stable upright posture: If he pushes or pulls your upper body from over your hips, you are more likely to fall down. So during the physical struggle with the attacker, in order to keep your hips under your head, you need to do *step-and-drag stepping*.

Step-and-drag stepping is the same movement as step and drive, except that instead of stepping with the foot that's closest to the direction you want to go and then driving your weight off the other foot, you step with the closest foot and then drag the other foot on its ball to bring your feet to a comfortable position. Step-and-drag stepping ensures that you always have both feet on the ground in a pyramid base foot position.

If an attacker pulls at you, step-and-drag forward toward him so you don't losing your balance. If he pushes you backward, step-and-drag back to keep from losing your balance to the rear and being knocked over.

In spite of your best efforts you may end up on the ground. If you do go down, swivel on your buttocks so that your feet are facing your attacker, and try to kick his legs and knees. As soon as there's room, get back on your feet. Being on the ground is very disadvantageous: It's very tiring, and even a person well trained in ground fighting has a very limited amount of time before his or her strength runs out. This is why, in police training, we say "If you're on the ground and aren't hand-cuffing the subject, then you're losing!"

By doing step-and-drag stepping, you'll be more likely to keep an assailant from knocking you down. Remember that the longer you can keep the assailant struggling with you, the greater the risk he has of being seen, and of someone's coming to your aid, or of your escaping.

If you feel that someone is following or coming toward you:

1. Run to your escape route. Keep running away from the attacker until you feel safe.
2. Then find help, such as a police officer, a security officer, or some other authority figure.

If you know that you are definitely being followed and see an attacker coming toward you:

1. Shout at the person to "Stay back!" Simultaneously run to your escape route.
2. While running, yell "Help! Help! Fire! Fire!"

If you haven't identified a clear escape route, you may have to:

1. Turn toward the assailant and assume a defensive stance.
2. Raise your reaction hand toward the subject to keep him an arm's length away as you shout "Stop! Back! Stop! Back!"
3. If you can, immediately look for an escape route and run to it. Begin shouting "Help! Help! Fire! Fire!"

These patterns of movement, simple though they be, are the foundation for getting away from an attacker. They must be practiced until you can do them comfortably, without having to think about them.

How to Deal With
a Violent Confrontation

STOP THE ASSAULT
AND THEN GET AWAY

STEP 5
STOP THE ASSAULT
AND THEN GET AWAY

Your ultimate objective is to get away from your assailant without engaging him physically and, if that's not immediately possible, to get to a position that's more to your advantage if you need to fight. Hopefully you will avoid confrontation entirely, or escape and reach safety, or someone will hear you and come to your aid. Unfortunately, you can't rely on any of these things happening, and you may not be able to avoid a confrontation. If this is the case, you will need realistic, practical, and effective options that will allow you to stop the assailant's attack and incapacitate him long enough for you to get away.

In Step 5 you will learn to combine simple but effective hand-to-hand combat techniques with the use of emergency safety tools. There is a wide range of emergency safety tools available, and, hopefully, one will fit your needs.

Hand-to-hand combat skills are extremely simple movements far removed from martial arts films. They're probably already more familiar than you think, especially the ones that we'll be sharing with you, such as a slap, or a kick to the attacker's leg, or a knee to his stomach.

Emergency Safety Tools and the Law

The tools we discuss in this step are considered weapons by the legal system, which is concerned about citizens misusing weapons. Each jurisdiction has its own laws governing those tools, so it is *imperative* that you check with your local law enforcement authority about carrying and using any emergency safety tool. We are not attorneys, and we can not and do not provide legal advice. You *must* check with local, state, and federal authorities about whether you can carry a particular emergency safety tool, and you *must* comply with all appropriate laws. These laws can and do vary greatly from jurisdiction to jurisdiction.

As a rule of thumb, as a civilian you *always*, like the knights in *Monty Python and the Holy Grail*, want to "Run away! Run away!" if possible. This is especially true if you have a weapon, whose mere presence gives you added responsibility.

We cannot overemphasize how important it is to avoid a confrontation, independent of the provocation, if you can safely do so.

As an example, if someone says "Your mother wears army boots" and you respond "Your father wears a mustache" and he comes back with a snappy "So's your old man" and the next thing you know there's a fight, then *you* will be given a big share of the responsibility for what happened, since *you* kept the ball rolling. This is clearly a case where being macho can cause you problems.

The Confrontational Continuum

What levels of force are there, anyway, and how can you respond to them? This is an important consideration, because police and lawyers analyzing an incident will give close scrutiny to whether force was used *maliciously to cause bodily injury*, or *in good faith to control, restrain, and subdue.*

Remember that force can be deescalated as well as escalated. This means you must make an effort to avoid and retreat from the conflict if possible, and should think out the ramifications of using force beforehand, rather than after the fact.

It is critical from both an ethical and a legal point of view that, if you use force, you be able to verbalize why the level of force you used was appropriate. To understand use of force more clearly, let's look, from the perspective of law enforcement, at the escalating continuum of *resistance and control* used on both sides of a confrontation: This is the context from which the police will look at your use of force.

Levels of Resistance

Resistance—which is assault from your point of view—moves up a scale of increasing likelihood of your attacker causing you physical harm. Resistance (assault) falls into four broad areas:

1. Verbal dialogue (including psychological intimidation by the assailant, and verbal noncompliance to your directions).

2. Resistive actions (passive, even if threatening).
3. Aggressive acts (you are being physically touched and assaulted, or it is clear that you are about to be assaulted, such as when someone appears and yells "Give me your money!").
4. Aggravated active aggression (your attacker is trying to kill or severely injure you).

As a civilian, you have the right to physically defend yourself against aggressive acts and aggravated active aggression.

Levels of Control

Control—which is self-defense from your point of view—moves up a scale of increasing likelihood of you causing your attacker physical harm:

1. Presence (folks behave differently when there's a cop around, or when you behave alertly and with authority).
2. Verbal direction (saying what you want done, with the expectation that your orders will be followed).
3. Empty-hand control (including punching, kicking, martial arts, personal defense sprays[9], and other defensive techniques).

---

9. While personal defense sprays sound more like intermediate weapons than empty hand control, they are included at this level because they cause less harm than punching someone.

4. Intermediate weapons (such as nightsticks and defensive keychains).
5. Deadly force (any force that would cause death or grave bodily harm, even if that harm won't actually kill your attacker).

What Should You Use to Protect Yourself?

Physical Skills

Martial Arts

If you're young and strong (and watch too much television), the idea of martial arts or some other form of physical skill for self-defense is appealing. Unfortunately, use of martial arts for self-defense presents four problems:

First, martial arts require a near life-long dedication to be effective, even in training sessions.

Second, they are arts, and are not generally aimed at dealing with the kinds of attacks that happen on the street.

Third, the techniques are often taught by artists, not fighters, without reference to the realities of combat, and may not prepare you psychologically or emotionally for confrontation. Indeed, you may go through years of training without actually being struck by an opponent.

Finally, all things being equal, since professional predators generally attack only people they think they can defeat, a predator will attack you only if he is larger than you (or for some other reason thinks he can control you). The larger, younger, stronger person has the advantage in a physical confrontation—that's why every sport from boxing to judo separates competitors by weight, and sometimes also by age.[10]

When you combine all these factors, it's no surprise that Kleck indicates that if you use physical force to counter a robbery you have only a 49.2% chance of remaining unhurt, and that if you use physical force to counter an assault you have only a 47.9% chance of remaining unhurt. What this means is that if you *do* decide to fight back, what you do *must* work for you to remain safe.

While the martial arts require engagement, the techniques discussed in this book have as their aim *avoidance of* and *escape from* engagement. Our interest is survival and safety, not in demonstrating fancy moves. It is important for readers—especially men—to understand that winning does not always mean getting into a fight.

The Seven Steps to Personal Safety[sm]

An exception to "larger-wins" is the program—based on this book—that is available from instruc-

---

10. On the other hand, spending a month or so studying a martial art such as Aikido—which makes little pretense of being a good choice for self-defense—can help you learn to recognize an impending attack, get out of the way, and move well.

tors certified through the ASR Instructors Council. The program is either a half-day course which includes lecture and training in the use of personal defense sprays, or a full-day course which includes lecture and training in the use of personal defense sprays and defensive keychains. Like this book, these courses emphasize avoidance of confrontation. We believe the Seven Steps[sm] program is the fastest way for the normal person to develop adequate personal safety skills and techniques.

The IMPACT[sm] Program

A second exception to "larger-wins" is the IMPACT[sm] program. This, too, is not a martial art, but a 20-hour program which teaches women to fight all-out against attackers. We are given to understand that this program was developed when it was realized that female martial artists were losing fights in the street.

A significant goal of the program is to help students realize that nobody has the right to assault them, and that they have the right to defend themselves—in essence, The Decision. The program develops a realistic sense of confidence and competence through street-realistic scenarios; trainers wear protective gear, permitting full-contact fighting on the part of the student. This role-playing generates great stress, which in turn allows the release of focused adrenalin strength (the kind of strength one sees when a mother picks up a 2,000-pound automobile to save her child).

IMPACT^{sm}—and similar programs—supply a valid feeling of empowerment and the confidence that comes from good technique. It is an excellent, albeit stressful, program, highly recommended for all girls and women.

Emergency Safety Tools

The next appealing idea is some sort of defensive weapon which can be used as an emergency safety tool. Tools are critical, since your ability to exert maximum effort will last no more than 20 to 45 seconds before you run out of short-term endurance. For most people this means using a gun, a knife, a personal defense spray, or a club.

Guns

Guns are terrific safety tools, as shown by the fact that Americans use a gun about 2,500,000 times each year to stop a crime.[11] According to Kleck, if you use a gun to defend yourself in a robbery, you have a 74.8% chance of being unhurt; in an assault, the chance of being uninjured rises to 87.5%. While this seems no better than doing nothing in a robbery, it is better in an assault.[12]

---

11. Kleck and Gertz, preliminary study, 1993
12. We think that these figures are a little misleading, since we believe that the mere suspicion that a gun is present will make a predator go elsewhere, thus reducing the number of attacks.

There are, however, some problems with guns. For a start, guns bring with them a responsibility commensurate with their power, and many people won't (and some people can't) accept the responsibility and are frightened by the power. This, coupled with the fact that the level of risk in day-to-day living for most people is extremely low, makes a gun an inappropriate choice for most of us as an emergency safety tool.

In addition, you have to carry a gun with you all the time in order to have it the one time you need it, and in some states and cities this is, incredibly, not legally possible. And guns, particularly long guns, are heavy, bulky, uncomfortable, and annoyingly inconvenient to carry.

The bottom line is that while in this country there are more guns than automobiles, while a gun is used every 12.6 seconds by a private citizen to stop a crime, while there is a gun in over half of all households, while 12.5% of women now have a gun, while more people engage in gun sports than play tennis, while 1 out of every 27 civilians does carry a gun on a regular basis, and while some consider ownership of a gun to be an obligation of good citizenship much like voting or participating in civic and community activities, neither author of this book feels impelled to keep or carry a gun for personal defense or protection, and guns most likely will not fit in with either your lifestyle or your perception of risk.

Finally, since two out of every three gun deaths are suicides, it is inappropriate to have a gun in the house if there is a depressed teenager—or adult for that matter—with access to the gun. This will not prevent their suicide: It is well established that suicide rates are independent of tools available, and a person who plans to commit suicide will do so whether or not there is a gun around. Nonetheless, if you don't keep a gun in the house you will be at least relieved of the additional guilt you would feel if someone you love were to use your gun as the instrument of his or her death.

If, however, you do choose to own a gun for self-protection in spite of all these considerations, you must consider the question of training. Training is very important—power brings with it responsibility, and a gun has great power. You need three types of training:

First and foremost, you must have training in *gun safety and use.* Courses in gun safety are offered nationwide under the auspices of the National Rifle Association.

Second, you need training in the *legal and moral aspects* of using a gun. To learn about this critical area we urge anyone owning a gun to read *In the Gravest Extreme: The Role of the Firearm in Personal Protection* by Massad Ayoob (Concord, N. H.: Police Bookshelf, 1983).

Third, you need training in *combat shooting*— as opposed to target, practical, or sport shooting.

These courses deal with developing the mindset, decision-making skill, and tactics needed to use a gun under the stress of a violent confrontation.

Knives

Knives might seem appealing in the movies, but in real life are infinitely less so in virtually every respect. Knives are looked on with distaste by a significant portion of the population: Nice people—the kind who serve on juries—don't carry knives with which to cut other people. Knives are very difficult to defend in court because they are not used as defensive tools by police. Also, knives require very close personal contact in order to be effective. According to Kleck, if you use a knife to defend yourself against a robbery you face a 59.7% chance of being uninjured, and in an assault you face a 70.5% chance of being uninjured. This is notably worse than doing nothing in a robbery, though about the same as doing nothing in an assault. We do not recommend that knives be carried for personal safety.

Personal Defense Sprays

Much like the six-shooter of the Old West, personal defense sprays should be the great equalizer, with the advantage of being nonlethal. And, as of this printing, they are generally legal for civilian use everywhere but in New York. You must, of course, check all local, state, and federal laws to see what restrictions apply where you are.

There are at present over 100 personal defense sprays on the market, some good, with a near-zero failure-to-control rate with trained use, and some not so good, with up to a 60% failure-to-control rate for untrained users. How can you tell which are good and which are not so good? Without testing in the field on pain-resistant subjects it's hard to know for sure, but most major manufacturers of personal defense sprays for law enforcement also make civilian versions. The firearms instructor at your local police department should be able to give you some guidance as to which products are not only widely carried, but also have a successful track record.

Note that while being sprayed yourself is an unforgettable experience, it actually gives no indication of how the product would work against a pain-resistant attacker—unless, of course, you yourself are drunk, on drugs, or crazy.

There are two general classes of personal defense sprays, which will be described below. The first is *teargas* and the second is *aerosol subject restraints (ASRs)*. Teargas has, perhaps because of its military origin, traditionally been considered within law enforcement to be an intermediate weapon used at the same level of force as a nightstick. Some agencies, however, have recently begun to place teargas lower on the force continuum.

It might seem logical that an aerosol subject restraint would also be considered an intermediate weapon, like teargas. However, because of early wide recognition of its extremely low propensity to cause lasting injury (less injury than might be caused by hitting someone), the law-enforcement community generally considers its use to be on the *same* level of force as merely restraining someone with your empty hands when he is noncompliant and expected to fight back, and on a *lower* level of force than hitting someone with your fists, forearms, elbows, knees, or feet.

There are two factors—other than training—that are important in a personal defense spray. The first is the *distance* at which it can be used. When you spray an attacker with a personal defense spray, it should project out of the canister in a form that allows it to be used close up. This is very important because *virtually all uses of personal defense sprays take place within a yard or less* (arm's length or closer). A properly designed personal defense spray has no minimum required distance to prevent mechanical injury from the pressure of the spray. If you had to, you should, with proper technique, be able to spray an assailant directly in the face even at point-blank range—certainly closer than one foot—and get full effect without putting out your assailant's eye.

The minimum distance a personal defense spray will reach depends on the model, size, and spray pattern of the dispenser. Some personal defense sprays project in a coherent stream (primarily teargas, which will *sublimate*, with the rising vapors being inhaled). Streams have the advantage of being relatively unaffected by wind. Others—primarily ASRs, which do not sublimate—project in a cone-of-mist. Mists have the advantage of allowing the atomized ASR to be breathed in directly, but are affected by the wind. Still others come out in a burst designed to reach great distances. It doesn't matter what type of dispenser is used as long as the product can be used close up. Check the product's instruction sheet to make sure the spray can be used at arms length or closer. If not, get a different personal defense spray.

Maximum distance, on the other hand, is of no real concern. A personal defense spray will virtually always be used against an assailant who is within arm's length of you. It's *extremely* unlikely that you will have any opportunity to use a personal defense spray at any distance beyond six feet. So anything beyond six feet is pretty much wasted spray.

The second factor is the duration of spray. Since you don't want to run out of spray before you run out of confrontation, there should be a *minimum* of 10 seconds' total continuous discharge (TCD) for a personal defense spray—if you press on the actuator, a useful amount of spray should come out for at least 10 seconds. You can find out the total continuous discharge time from the manufacturer. The TCD is a more reliable indicator of how long the can will last than an estimate of the number of one-second sprays in the dispenser.

A third factor that may be of consideration in the winter is whether the propellant is effective at very low temperatures. The manufacturer can give you the temperature range for which his product has proven effective. Or, to test this yourself, put a dispenser in the freezer overnight. Then take it quickly outside and see if it sprays well.

Read the manufacturer's instructions regarding use, storage, and safe handling of the particular personal defense spray you choose to carry.

Teargas: CN   Following World War I, a chemical agent called CN was adopted by law enforcement. Its finely ground particles hurt the eyes and caused tearing (thus the name teargas). It had mild effects, but was supposedly strong enough to incapacitate for a short period.

One problem with personal defense sprays that have CN as their sole active ingredient is that CN works by causing pain. Anyone who is highly enraged, psychotic, well trained, or on drugs or alcohol will, in most cases, be oblivious to pain. When CN does work, its *onset time*—the time required until controlling effect begins—is short, and so it works quickly. But, unfortunately, it's so mild that it is often ineffective against a pain-resistant person. Law enforcement and the military have gotten mixed results with CN, and, though CN has been widely carried, it is rarely used.

Read the label before you buy a personal defense spray. If CN is the only active ingredient, we suggest that you *don't* buy it.

Teargas: CS By the late 1950s the United States military dropped its use of CN for a newly developed teargas called CS. By the mid-1960s CS was adopted by American law enforcement agencies as the riot-control agent of choice. Both the U.S. military and law enforcement agencies changed to CS because it worked better than CN. It caused the eyes to close, produced heavy tearing, coughing, a feeling of panic, and sometimes nausea or vomiting, and disorientation and confusion. Once an assailant has been properly sprayed with CS and it has taken effect, it will prevent the resumption of further aggressive activity for up to 30 minutes.

A well-formulated CS will work virtually all the time, even on pain-resistant subjects. But on truly pain-resistant subjects—those who are drunk, on drugs, or psychotic—it *can*, depending on the formulation, take 20 to 60 seconds for the full effect to kick in. This might make some formulations inappropriate for spontaneous defense.

Most CS defense sprays are packaged in canisters that shoot the product out in a narrow stream. This *may* require a minimum safe distance for spraying, and—as with a total continuous discharge time of under 10 seconds—may disqualify particular dispensers from consideration. In addition, you should make sure that the CS you choose is a brand designed for and widely used by police.

Aerosol Subject Restraints (ASRs): Capsaicin Animal-control sprays based on capsaicin have been available for a long time—often in the form of oleoresin capsicum (OC), which is derived from New World red peppers not much different from the hot peppers used in cooking and which is environmentally sound. In 1973 a commercially viable capsaicin-based personal defense spray hit the marketplace. It was not actively marketed and remained virtually unknown until it was introduced to the law enforcement community at the 1988 conference of the American Society of Law Enforcement Trainers by one of the authors of this book. The effect of this class of personal defense spray on pain-resistant subjects was generally immediate on contact, so it was extremely effective in spontaneous defense, where the attack is unexpected and must be dealt with immediately. It so captured the attention, interest, and approval of the law enforcement community that by 1990 other manufacturers began making similar products.

Capsaicin-based products are *inflammatory agents*, and work by inflaming the mucous membranes. They do not work by affecting the central nervous system, as do the irritants used in teargas. This is important because inflammation of tissues is a very low-level physiological response, and is unaffected by factors such as training, stress, drugs, alcohol, psychosis, goal-orientation, or any other form of pain resistance. And although not designed or intended for animal control, they have been reported to work on dogs and other domestic animals, zoo animals, and wild animals.

Because of the way capsaicin-based products work, this class of emergency safety tools is categorized as an *aerosol subject restraint,* or *ASR,* rather than as a teargas. An aerosol subject restraint[13] is a generic class of personal defense sprays whose sole active ingredient is capsaicin.

An ASR—whether in stream, cone-of-mist, or burst units—will dilate the capillaries of the subject's eyelids, causing the eyes to close temporarily. The subject's eyes and vision are not actually affected. It is merely that the eyelids are clamped shut for a brief period of time. Since, for sighted people, the greater portion of our contact with the world is visual, this can be a significant control factor for all but the most hardened cases.

In addition, when a mist of atomized ASR is inhaled it temporarily inflames the mucous membranes of the throat. This induces a bout of uncon-

---

13. As an historical aside, the term "aerosol subject restraint" was coined by William J. McCarthy of Indianapolis to differentiate ASRs from teargas, and quickly entered into the general law enforcement lexicon.

trollable coughing which both causes the subject to double over at the waist and produces a temporary loss of muscular strength and coordination.

The closed eyes, combined with the uncontrollable coughing, drastically reduces your attacker's desire and ability to continue fighting, and affects even the most hardened cases.

With proper use, an ASR will prevent the resumption of further aggressive activity for up to 30 minutes.

As with any personal defense spray, you should consider whether a specific product can be used at close range and has a minimum total continuous discharge of 10 seconds.

Teargas: Teargas/Oleoresin Capsicum Blends
Some manufacturers have recently started to produce personal defense sprays containing teargas (CN or CS) blended with oleoresin capsicum (OC). The intention with the blends is that the OC will immediately close the subject's eyes, buying time until the CN or CS kicks in. The teargas/OC blends have been well received and seem promising based on anecdotal reports from police use.

A teargas/oleoresin capsicum blend is considered to be teargas, not an ASR. As with any personal defense spray, you should check that a specific blend can be used at close range, and that it has a minimum total continuous discharge of at least 10 seconds.

Impact Weapons and Defensive Keychains

Impact weapons are simply nightsticks, clubs, or bludgeons. These are illegal in most jurisdictions, and even if you try to be clever by having, say, a baseball bat on the front seat of your car, it's likely to be frowned on by the police.

A nice malacca or Irish blackthorn walking stick might seem appropriate, but, in truth, few people carry canes today. Also, proper use of a cane for self-defense is more like using a sword than a club, and it's very difficult to get proper training. And if you end up whacking someone over the head with a cane you will very probably be charged with illegal possession and use of a club.

A special subset of the club is the defensive keychain used in police work. Defensive keychains are small cylinders generally made of plastic or metal. The barrel is about six inches long and about half an inch wide, with keys on a ring at one end. The design of defensive keychains varies somewhat among manufacturers—some are a little thicker or thinner, some have grooves and some have ridges, and some telescope open an additional few inches—but they're all used the same way. Defensive keychains have proven themselves to be effective safety tools in police work, are completely legal for civilian possession in most jurisdictions, and are included as one of the emergency safety tools taught in the full-day *Seven Steps to Personal Safety*^{sm} training program.

In police work, defensive keychains are used with a set of compression, leverage, and counter-strike techniques to gain statutory control, and are considered to be higher on the force continuum than empty-hand control, but lower on the force continuum than hitting someone.

For civilian use against a violent attack, the techniques use the higher-level force of strikes and slashes to the face and other vulnerable areas. Striking someone as hard as you can in the face, eyes, nose, mouth, or throat with the keys on the end of a defensive keychain can cause great bodily harm. And force that can cause death or great bodily harm is considered deadly force. Because of this, civilian use of the defensive keychain is at the same level of force as other impact weapons, and much higher on the force continuum than personal defense sprays or empty-hand techniques. **The only justification for using defensive force of this magnitude on another person is that you face the imminent likelihood of death or grave bodily harm from that person!**

Even though the use of a defensive keychain is a viable option to stop a violent attack, and even though it is used at a higher level of force than a personal defense spray, the personal defense spray should still be your primary emergency safety tool. This is because even if you hit an attacker in the face so hard that you put out his eye or rip off part of his nose, he may still be able—because of pain-resistance brought on by a rush of adrenalin, or drink, or drugs, or training, or just plain craziness—to fight through the pain. After all, many criminals have been mortally wounded in police gunfights, only to continue to fight back for minutes that seemed like hours.

Therefore, we recommend that you use a defensive keychain only in situations where you can't use a personal defense spray, or to buy you time to access your personal defense spray.

Using Emergency Safety Tools

By a stroke of good fortune, all safety tools are used in a very similar way: First, you avoid the immediate threat—referred to in police work as "exiting the kill zone," that area, usually directly in front of the attacker, where you face the greatest danger. Second, you verbally "stun" your attacker. Third, you execute the technique for that safety tool. And finally, you leave to get help.

Because they are the easiest to describe in written form, are the easiest to learn from a book because they depend on gross motor skills, and are legal almost everywhere, we will spend the rest of this step dealing with the use of personal defense sprays and defensive keychains: We recommend that you carry both, so that if someone snatches your keys you still have your spray. But remember that techniques not directly peculiar to the use of personal defense sprays or defensive keychains are applicable to other emergency safety tools.

There are a few rules you should be aware of when using or carrying any emergency safety tool:

1. An emergency safety tool is a defensive weapon, not a toy. Don't play with it!
2. Don't let people know you are carrying an emergency safety tool. It's none of their business, and could cause you harm.
3. Don't use an emergency safety tool as a threat. Thus, if you carry a personal defense spray, don't say "Stop, or I'll spray:" If you have time to talk, you should either be spraying or taking some other action. Also, you're likely to be disarmed before you finish speaking, since most of us can't act and talk at the same time.
4. Use of an emergency safety tool should come as a surprise to your attacker, which will make it all the more effective.
5. Federal law prohibits the carrying of weapons, including personal defense sprays and defensive keychains, on airplanes.
6. You should not discharge a personal defense spray in or from a moving vehicle, or on public transport, since the vehicle could go out of control and wreak havoc.
7. You are responsible for your actions, particularly in public places, and your use of an emergency safety tool must err on the side of safety.

8. If you have an emergency safety tool, you have an increased obligation and responsibility to walk away from a confrontation if it is physically and morally possible to do so.

It is important to remember that this book does not take the place of proper training in the use of a personal defense spray, a defensive keychain, or any other emergency safety tool. Approved certification training for personal defense sprays should be available through the product's manufacturer. However, at the time of writing all three major manufacturers of law enforcement personal defense sprays recognize the training program based on this book, which is offered nationwide through the Center for Personal Defense Studies.

Techniques and Tactics

You go to Step 5 only if you have not been able to get away. Your goal is to stop your attacker's forward momentum and then incapacitate him with your emergency safety tool. You can then escape from the assailant and run for help.

You should realize from the start that an escalation in your actions may generate an escalation in the attacker's response, and that no technique works 100% of the time. Only you can determine the acceptability and risk of fighting versus not fighting once it is clear that you can't get away.

Exiting the Kill Zone

If the subject continues to move toward you, exit the "kill zone" by moving to the right or left if there is space. Think of an attacker as a train rolling down the track toward you. You want to *get off the track* rather than try to outrun the train. Let the attacker end up where you were, while you end up to his side, or even back where he was when he started moving.

Verbal Stunning

Studies have shown that when individuals are experiencing a heightened level of stress and anxiety, they don't hear well *what* is being said to them. They only hear *how* it's being said. *How* you say what you say, therefore, must match the action and intensity of *what* you are saying, so you must use loud repetitive verbal commands.

As the assailant is coming toward you, verbally "stun" your attacker with loud repetitive verbal commands like "Stop! Stay back!" or "Back!" Your commands must be assertive ultimatums and not passive pleading such as "Don't hurt me" or "What do you want?" Use verbal stunning to demonstrate that you are in charge and in control.

Simultaneously, spray or strike him in the face until he has stopped assaulting you, all the time shouting such verbal commands as "Stop! Down!" or "Down! Down! Down!" Verbal stunning is very important, particularly after the subject has been sprayed with a personal defense spray or struck with a defensive keychain, because he will be in a state of confusion and will be seeking instructions. The instructions you want him to follow are the ones you are giving him with your verbal stunning.

Distraction and Distance-Creation Techniques

It may be, however, that you can't spray or strike the assailant without first stopping his initial charge. You will need to use a *distraction technique*, which will bring him up short, taking advantage of the element of surprise. Distraction techniques are intended to create time and distance in which to spray, or to strike with your defensive keychain. If you are grabbed from behind while your personal defense spray or defensive keychain is in your hand, don't drop it. At some point you should have an opportunity to spray or to strike your attacker.

Brachial Stun

The brachial stun is a slap to the side of the neck with the palm or back of your open hand, or with the soft inside or back of your wrist. This excites the brachial plexus nerve complex, momentarily stunning your attacker. It needs **under six pounds** of force, and you can safely try it on yourself.

From a stable pyramid base foot position, quickly smack the side of of the assailant's neck while shouting "Stop!" Let your hand or wrist stay in contact with the neck for about an eighth of a second, rather than bouncing off: this will allow the maximum amount of energy to be transferred.

If you can, break away and run for help. Try to step and drag to the outside of the assailant by going to his right or left as you simultaneously spray or strike him in the eyes, nose, and mouth. Keep spraying or striking until the assailant stops assaulting you, then break away.

Multi-Strike Forearm Overload

As the attacker moves in toward you (as you're facing him), shove your reaction hand into his chest—or extend both hands to forcefully check his forward motion—and command him to "Stay back!" If he continues to press in toward you, bring your hands into your chest, making fists with your hands and putting your fists together, palms facing down and touching your chest.

Begin striking him with the elbow end of your forearms. You must involve your whole body in the strikes, using hip and upper body motion so he is receiving the force of your entire body weight. Do multiple rapid strikes, as hard as you can, alternating forearms, to his chest and upper body as you shout "Stop! Back!"

If grabbed from behind, and your arms aren't pinned to your sides, do a reverse multi-strike overload with the elbow end of your upper arms. Do multiple rapid strikes backward, alternating arms as you shout "Stop! Back!" Get away if you can. Otherwise spray or strike your assailant in the face and then break away.

Punch to Stomach

Using either hand, even if the hand isn't empty, punch the assailant as hard and as fast as you can in the middle of his stomach and command him "Stop!" This could knock the wind out of him. If you can, get away then. Otherwise, spray or strike him and then break away.

Forearm Strike

Alternatively, bring a hand to the center of your chest and strike your attacker in the upper body or face and head with your forearm, as in the multi-strike forearm overload. If you can, get away. Otherwise, spray or strike him then break away.

Knee Strike

A knee strike can be performed with either knee, depending on your position. Extend one or both hands out and grab your opponent. Simultaneously, as the assailant presses in, pull him in toward you. Shift your body weight over your hip and bring your other hip and knee up to form a spear with your knee: The heel of your foot should be touching your buttocks by the time your knee strikes. Drive your knee into the center of his stomach as you simultaneously command him "Stop!" You may have to bring the leg back to the floor and do several knee strikes before you can break away.

The stomach is a better target than the groin: First, it's a bigger target area and easier to hit. Second, a knee in the stomach will cause more immediate incapacitation than will a knee to the groin. Third, most men are very good at protecting their groin, and the attacker may be able to block a knee coming toward his groin.

Kick

If you have time, drive the ball of your foot into the assailant's shin or knee as he is moving in toward you. Command the assailant to "Stop!"

Using the Personal Defense Spray

We have been talking about spraying the subject in the eyes, nose, and mouth with your personal defense spray. As easy as this sounds, there's more to it than just pointing and spraying. While it seems as if you should be able to just "point and spray" or "follow the bouncing head," police use of personal defense sprays has shown that effective spraying, combined with appropriate verbalization while simultaneously avoiding the attack, is a psychomotor skill that requires training.

In addition, you need to give some thought as to where to carry your personal defense spray, how to draw it, how to hold it in your weapon hand, how to fire it, and how to ensure hitting the target at which you're aiming.

Carrying the Personal Defense Spray
In the Hand

In the best of all possible worlds, your personal defense spray would be in your weapon hand at all times when you might be at risk. To make this more likely, if you follow our recommendation to carry your keys on a defensive keychain, you should develop the habit of picking up your personal defense spray whenever you pick up your keys. If you don't carry a defensive keychain, you should purchase a personal defense spray that has a belt clip and a keyring at the bottom for your keys. This way, wherever your keys are, your personal defense spray is.

You can add a device that allows you to detach the keys, so that the personal defense spray will still be available when the keys are physically in the lock. Alternatively, if your keys are in the lock when you're attacked, you'll have to pull on the holster to detach it from the keys (i.e., rip the dispenser away from the keys).

Make sure you can tell—by feel—which is the front: It would be embarrassing at the least and dangerous at the worst to spray yourself. The clip will provide a positive tactile indicator.

As you carry the personal defense spray—concealed in your weapon hand—make sure that as soon as you perceive a threat, you place your thumb on the personal defense spray's actuator. This way you'll be ready to spray without having to fumble around.

You should have the personal defense spray in your hand any time you feel uncomfortable with your surroundings. Since most personal defense sprays are small enough to fit in the palm of your hand, concealing them from plain view, it's good practice to have it in your hand going to or from your car, coming toward the door when returning home, in elevators, in deserted public transportation exits, in parking lots, and any other place where you might feel at risk.

Have your personal defense spray in your hand, not in your purse, and keep it in your hand when you get out of your car—don't be too quick to put it away.

If you feel that someone is following you, have your personal defense spray in your hand, ready to fire. Stop and turn toward him so you can see what he is doing and choose the appropriate plan of action. If it's night and you have a high intensity flashlight—in your reaction hand—shine your flashlight toward his eyes and blind him with the light. Then look for his hands and palms to see if he is holding any weapons.

The best defense against being assaulted is awareness—keep the mind alert and thinking at all times.

In the Pocket

Carrying the personal defense spray in a jacket or coat pocket is acceptable as long as it doesn't get caught or hung up when you're trying to draw it in a high-stress situation. For the greatest safety, carry your personal defense spray only in a very large and unrestrictive pocket. You can use the clip to hold it in a secure position.

In a Carrying Bag or Purse

If you carry your personal defense spray in a bag or purse, it should be easily accessible so that it can be drawn when you're under stress. Use the clip to attach it to the bag in a place that's easy to find. Don't just dump it in a bag or purse with all the stuff you have in there: You may end up drawing out a brush or wallet instead of the personal defense spray. If your bag or purse has an open side pocket (inside or outside), that's a good place to put it—alone.

On the Belt

If you use a clip to attach the personal defense spray to your belt, the personal defense spray should be *concealed*, rather than publicly displayed. Public display will make some good people uncomfortable, and will eliminate the element of surprise with bad people who mean you harm.

Drawing the Personal Defense Spray

If you carry the personal defense spray in your weapon hand, it's already drawn and ready to go.

If you draw it from a bag, purse, or pocket, you may need your reaction hand to turn it in your weapon hand so that the spray nozzle is pointed in the right direction. You should also practice being able to tell by feel which is the front, so you don't accidentally spray yourself.

Basic Positions

Weapon Hand While Walking or Running

Your personal defense spray can be concealed in your weapon hand as you walk or run to wherever you're going. Concealing the personal defense spray adds an element of surprise if you need to defend against an attack.

Ready Position

If you're confronted and feel threatened, you may want to further conceal your personal defense spray: Tuck your weapon hand, with your thumb on the actuator, slightly behind your weapon thigh as you turn your body by moving to a pyramid base, your weapon foot drawn back and turned out 60 degrees. The personal defense spray is in your weapon hand palm facing to the rear.

From here, you can move to the loaded or firing positions.

Loaded Position

If the person is practically on top of you, you may need to move into a position that unfortunately lets the assailant see that you have a defensive weapon.

In the loaded position, you are going from the ready position (carrying the personal defense spray in your weapon hand and at your side as you are running or walking) to a position in which you bring your weapon hand up tight against your weapon side next to your chest and rib cage. Your thumb is on the actuator and the nozzle is pointing toward the assailant. Your reaction hand and arm are shoved out in front of you to keep the assailant at least at arm's length as you spray. You should also be in a wide and deep pyramid base foot position, with your weapon foot to the rear.

This loaded position is primarily a means of protecting the personal defense spray from being grabbed while you spray, since you're keeping the assailant back with your reaction hand. Also, if the attacker is so close and jammed into you that you can't go into the firing position, you'll have no choice but to discharge the personal defense spray from this loaded position, with your extended reaction hand creating distance.

This position *may* act as a psychological deterrent to the attacker, since it shows that you're armed with a weapon and are trained and prepared to use it. Because many predators are risk-aversive, this may be a help. However, this position is *not* intended as a deterrent: If you are forced into the loaded position you should be actively spraying, since you've now shown the assailant what you have. This could provide him with a means of countering your defense, especially since he's close enough to knock you down.

Firing Position

If your attacker is far enough away that he can't grab your extended hand, shove your weapon hand out at shoulder height. The extra distance will help protect you from getting the spray blown back if there's any wind. Keeping both of your eyes open, spray the personal defense spray directly toward the subject's face as you simultaneously shout "Stay back!" If the aggression continues, continue your defensive action. If using an ASR which comes out in a cone of mist, creating a curtain of mist which your attacker must penetrate to reach you, don't advance into the mist after firing or you might be affected, too. Move to one side or the other to avoid firing directly into the wind. If some of the mist blows back at you, it will annoy you but it won't incapacitate you. If you are running away this shouldn't be a factor.

If you're facing the attacker and not able to get away, shove your reaction hand straight out to protect your weapon hand. Both your arms are extended straight out and your eyes are open so you don't lose sight of your target. The spray dispenser can move back toward the loaded position if necessary to keep it from being grabbed.

Personal Defense Spray Targets and Method of Discharge

A personal defense spray must be sprayed directly at the attacker, either blanketing his face in a mist or coating his face with a stream or burst. Your targets are the assailant's mouth, nose, and eyes. Once the aggression has been stopped, you should stop spraying. Legally, you *must* stop spraying when an assailant stops attacking you, since the threat has ended and you can get away.

Spray Patterns

When the subject is closing in on you, he won't just move toward you in a straight line. A study of the dynamics of assault reveals that an attacker does a lot of bobbing and weaving to get past your defenses. This means that the assailant's face, which is the *only* target for the personal defense spray, is moving around a lot. Experience with police has shown us that hitting the target without training is more difficult than you might imagine.

Hitting the eyes, nose, and mouth of this moving target can be done if you're using proper spray patterns. All of the spray patterns start from either the loaded or the firing position. The "secret" of spraying the attacker is that wherever his face goes, the spray goes. Remember, the target is the attacker's face.

There are five spray patterns to learn. We developed these spray patterns when we discovered in training police that, without the development of a specific set of psychomotor skills, the effectiveness of use of the product *under stress* was lowered. These "gross-motor movements" are very much of the *Karate Kid* "wax on, wax off" school, and each one is based on movements that you've already performed thousands of times. They are what we refer to as *double-tap* movements, since each movement allows repeated sprays at your assailant by virtue of the multiple passes of the dispenser past his face as the dispenser is moved.

In addition to increasing the likelihood of hitting the subject with stream dispensers, the spray patterns allow a misting ASR to be used at closer range than if you just pointed and sprayed. A static spray allows the mist to turn liquid when it hits the subject. While this will close the subject's eyes, he may not breath in the mist and thus may not double over and lose strength and coordination. The spray patterns reduce this tendency of mist dispensers to turn liquid, allowing constant atomization down to about eight inches. If you practice in front of a closed window or a large mirror with an *inert training canister*, you'll get a good feel for how fast and over what distance the misting dispenser must be moved for maximum effectiveness.

After the initial training, you should practice your skill techniques on a daily basis for a minute or so until you're comfortable with the techniques. Once you're trained, you can perform repetitions of the technique using a mental visualization of the attacker's movements, or practice in dream simulations while asleep, which we will be discussing in more detail later this step under "Creative Visualization and Dream Practice."

Horizontal Sweep

If the attacker is moving from side-to-side as he tries to come in at you, follow and spray his face by firing the personal defense spray in a side-to-side sweeping motion, left to right or right to left. Remember, the assailant's mouth, nose, and eyes are the targets.

Vertical Sweep

If the attacker is trying to elude your spray by squatting or ducking down, follow and spray his face by firing the personal defense spray in a down-and-up vertical sweeping motion.

Vertical Sweep—Serpentine

If the attacker is moving in an up-and-down motion, you may reflexively follow and spray his face with an upward and downward vertical sweep that forms an S-type movement.

110

Circular Sweep

For this spray technique, follow the attacker's face and fire the personal defense spray in a clockwise or counterclockwise circular sweeping motion. This is an excellent technique for surrounding the assailant with a curtain of mist.

Criss-Cross Sweep

If the attacker is making downward diagonal movements, follow and spray his face with a criss-cross movement, like printing the letter X. This spray technique is excellent for covering large areas as the attacker is moving in toward you.

Treatment After Being Sprayed

Products vary, so it is critical that you check the manufacturer's instructions regarding treatment after a subject is sprayed. In general, if you inadvertently spray yourself or someone else, the symptoms can be relieved by:

- Flushing the eyes with clear cool water.
- Exposing the face and body to flowing air.
- Washing hair, face, and hands with soap and cold water to get the spray off the body, and changing a shirt or other clothing if needed.

Left untreated, the effects of a personal defense spray should go away in 15 to 45 minutes. If the effects last longer than this, consult a physician.

Decontamination

Since products vary, it is critical that you check the manufacturer's instructions regarding decontamination of the area in which a personal defense spray has been discharged. In general, well-formulated personal defense sprays do not require any special decontamination. Normal ventilation should generally remove the spray within 30 to 45 minutes. This means that if you accidentally discharge it at home or someplace else, it will disperse with normal ventilation, and no cleanup is normally required. Any clothing that has been sprayed can be tossed in with the regular wash.

Personal Defense Spray Training Simulations

You have been learning how to carry the personal defense spray and how to fire it at the assailant. Now you need to practice so that the proper responses will be so burned into you that you do them under stress without thinking.

Becoming proficient in the spray techniques will require you to perform the following simulations—slowly at first, gradually building up speed, intensity, and complexity.

Practice with training units, available from the manufacturer of your personal defense spray. Training units fire just like live units but don't contain any active ingredients, so they won't incapacitate anyone in the process.

Level 1 Simulations

First practice moving into your two firing positions (loaded and firing—as discussed earlier in this "Using the Personal Defense Spray" section under "Basic Positions") from the three basic stances (conversational, ready, and defensive—as discussed in Step 4 in the "Physical Skills for Self-Defense" section under "Stationary Stances"). Practice moving into each of the positions at least 50 times. The training unit should be gripped in your weapon hand with your thumb on the actuator. Don't discharge the training unit yet.

Next, exit the kill zone by "getting off the track," moving to the side as if avoiding a rushing attacker. Simultaneously perform one of the five double-tap spray patterns in the air slowly and rhythmically, but don't discharge the training unit. Give appropriate loud, repetitive verbal commands as you practice.

Since you're doing three things at once (moving aside, spraying, and yelling), start slowly and work up to a faster pace.

Level 2 Simulations

Repeat the movements of Level 1 for each of the five double-tap spray patterns, but this time simultaneously fire the training unit. For example, if you are performing the horizontal sweep, move your weapon hand laterally left to right as you fire, and then come back right to left. You can hold down the actuator for the full time, or release the actuator each time you pass the assailant's face.

Give appropriate loud, repetitive verbal commands, and move "off the track," so all three actions take place simultaneously.

Level 3 Simulations

Level 3 simulations require the help of a training partner wearing a gas mask or a swimming mask, who moves in to assault you from various attack positions and with various movements.

As your partner moves in toward you, follow and spray his or her face with the training unit while verbalizing and moving to the side. You're not hitting the target if your partner's face mask is not dampened. If your personal defense spray dispenses a cone of mist, you're not doing the spray patterns vigorously enough if your partner's mask is dripping wet. If it dispenses a stream or burst, there will be little direct atomization, and your partner's mask *will* be dripping.

As you become proficient at spraying the face of your moving partner, continue integrating your patterns of movement to get away and run for help.

Dynamic Simulations

Finally, make up scenarios, little plays in which you stage a scene where things escalate until you are attacked and must defend yourself. Practice these with a training unit and a partner.

The dynamics of these scenarios will become almost identical to real-life conditions of an actual assault. To stimulate your imagination, we include here five simulations designed by Jack Strenges of the Palm Beach Sheriff's Office. Scenarios can be practiced indoors or outside. Use your imagination when role-playing!

1. You have just gotten out of your car in a parking lot at a mall. It is nighttime and the parking lot is well lit. It's close to closing time and you're in a hurry to make a quick purchase. As you walk through the mall, someone suddenly blocks your path and attempts to grab you from the front. You must:

    • Create distance and try to retreat as appropriate, planning your escape route.

    • Simultaneously, get your personal defense spray in your hand in proper firing position.

    • Use verbal commands to attract attention.

    • Discharge your personal defense spray using the appropriate spray technique.

    • Spray until your attacker has ceased aggressive activity or is on the ground.

    • Utilize your escape route, escape, and call the police.

2. A disgruntled customer confronts you at the office door, forcing his way inside, physically assaulting you. You must:

- Create distance and try to retreat to a corner or to where there are other people, planning your escape route.

- Simultaneously, get your personal defense spray in your hand in proper firing position.

- Use verbal commands to attract attention.

- Discharge your personal defense spray using the appropriate spray technique.

- Spray until your attacker has ceased aggressive activity or is on the floor.

- Utilize your escape route, escape, and call the police.

3. You are inside an elevator and waiting to get off, keys (and personal defense spray) in hand. The door opens and you are forced back inside by an ex-boyfriend. He menaces you and attempts to attack you. You must:

- Create distance; since most elevators are only eight feet by eight feet in size, back into a corner.

- Verbalize your "Stop! Back!" commands.

- Discharge your personal defense spray with an appropriate spray technique.

- Attempt to engage a floor button to stop at the next floor.

- Spray until your attacker has ceased aggressive activity or is on the floor of the elevator.

- Get out of the elevator as soon as the doors open, escape, and call the police.

4. Your attacker has knocked you to the ground. You must:

- Use verbal commands to attract attention.

- Try to get into a ground fighting position, keeping your back against a wall, tire, curb, or whatever is available to protect your spine, while planning your escape route and kicking at your attacker to keep him at bay.

- Simultaneously, get your personal defense spray in your hand in proper firing position.

- Discharge your personal defense spray using an appropriate spray technique.

- Spray until your attacker has ceased aggressive activity or is on the ground.

- Get up as quickly as possible and utilize your escape route, escape, and call the police.

5. You are jogging. Multiple attackers attempt to stop you. You must:

- Use verbal commands to attract attention.

- Simultaneously, get your personal defense spray in your hand in proper firing position.

- Discharge your personal defense spray using the appropriate spray technique at the most imminent attacker, and then the next, and the next.

- Spray until your attackers have ceased aggressive activity or are on the ground.

- Utilize your escape route, escape, and call the police.

Using the Defensive Keychain

We have told you to strike the subject in the eyes, nose, and mouth with your defensive keychain. As easy as this sounds, there's more to it than just swinging with your weapon hand. As with personal defense sprays, effective striking, combined with appropriate verbalization while simultaneously avoiding the attack, is a psychomotor skill that requires training.

In addition, there are other considerations, such as where to carry your defensive keychain, how to draw it, how to hold it in your weapon hand, how to strike with it, and finally, how to ensure hitting the target at which you're aiming. We recommend that you put your keys on your defensive keychain, and carry your personal defense spray separately. This allows you to have the personal defense spray in your hand—albeit your reaction hand—and accessible even when your keys are in the lock or if someone tries to grab them. Or to have the personal defense spray concealed in your hand when, for whatever reason, you don't want to be holding your keys.

Carrying the Defensive Keychain

As with the personal defense spray, there are a number of choices as to where to carry your defensive keychain.

In the Hand

If your keys are on your defensive keychain, the only time you might normally have it in your hand is when approaching or opening a door. In this case, the barrel will be in the palm of your weapon hand, and you will be using your reaction hand to pick out the appropriate key. Note that if you feel uncomfortable in a situation there is no reason not to have your defensive keychain in your hand: They are only keys, after all, not a weapon, so nobody will notice or get upset.

On the Belt

Most men and many women (depending on what they are wearing) carry the defensive keychain with the barrel stuck inside the waistband of their trousers, with the keys hanging out. Either side is acceptable, and you should choose what is most comfortable for you. You don't need to be as concerned with concealing the defensive keychain as you would be with a personal defense spray, since all you have showing are your keys.

In the Pocket

Carrying the defensive keychain in a jacket or coat pocket is acceptable as long as it doesn't get caught or hung up when you're trying to draw it out in a high-stress situation. For the greatest safety, carry your defensive keychain only in a very large and unrestrictive pocket.

In a Carrying Bag or Purse

If you carry your defensive keychain in a bag or purse, it should be easily accessible to be drawn under stressful conditions. Tuck it into a pocket in the bag in an accessible location. (Don't just dump it in a bag or purse with everything else. You may end up drawing out a brush or wallet instead of the defensive keychain.) If your bag or purse has an open pocket, that's a good place to put it—alone.

Drawing and Gripping the Defensive Keychain

If you're carrying the defensive keychain in your weapon hand, it's already drawn and ready to go. If you draw it from a bag, purse, or pocket, you may need your reaction hand to turn it in your weapon hand so that the keys are at the thumb end of your hand. If you draw it from your waistband, you can use your weapon hand to grasp the barrel with the keys at the thumb end of your hand, or grab the keys with your reaction hand and then grab the barrel with your weapon hand with the keys, as always, at the thumb end.

The defensive keychain is gripped by making a fist around the barrel, with your four fingers around the barrel and your thumb wrapped over your index and middle fingers. The barrel should be gripped in the middle, with barrel showing at the keyring end (where your thumb is) and the bottom of the keychain. This will allow you to strike with the keys or with the bottom of the keychain. Also, the extra barrel at the bottom should help reduce the chance that the keychain might slip through your (hopefully) vice-like grip.

Basic Positions
Weapon Hand While Walking or Running

The barrel is concealed in your weapon hand as you walk or run to wherever you're going. Even though it is not obviously a weapon—only the keys are showing—concealing it gives you the element of surprise if you need to defend yourself against an attack.

Ready Position

If you're confronted by an individual and feel threatened, you may want to further conceal your defensive keychain: Tuck your weapon hand slightly behind your weapon thigh as you turn your body by moving to a pyramid base, your weapon foot drawn back and turned out 60 degrees. The defensive keychain is in your weapon hand with your thumb at the keyring end, palm facing to the rear.

Loaded Position

Unlike a personal defense spray, where you may have some distance between you and your attacker, a defensive keychain *must* be used at close range. If you're confronted by an individual you believe to be a threat, you will need to assume a position that unfortunately lets the assailant see that you have a defensive weapon.

In the loaded position, you are going from the ready position (carrying the defensive keychain in your weapon hand at your side) to a position in which you bring your weapon hand up above your shoulder. Your thumb is at the keyring end. Your reaction hand and arm extend out in front of you to keep the assailant at arm's length as you strike. You should also be in a wide and deep pyramid base foot position, weapon foot to the rear.

This loaded position is the primary position from which you will be striking, while still keeping the assailant back with your reaction hand.

Defensive Keychain Targets

Your primary target is the center of your attacker's face: the assailant's mouth, nose, and eyes. Striking to the center of the face increases the probability of making contact with the face. Severe damage to the face, particularly the eyes, will generally greatly diminish your attacker's will to fight. If you can't strike the face, you may be able to strike your attacker in the throat by thrusting with the end of the defensive keychain. Once the aggression has been stopped, you should stop striking and escape. Legally, you *must* stop striking when an assailant stops attacking you, since the threat has ended and you can get away.

Physical Effects

Unlike using a personal defense spray, where the attacker will require no medical assistance, striking someone as hard as you can with a defensive keychain may result in grave bodily harm. If you strike your attacker in the face with your keys, you should expect the result to be anything from an abrasion to a large gaping wound with lots of blood rushing out. You may rip the attacker's eye out or tear his nose off. If you strike your attacker in the throat, you may crush, puncture, or severely damage his throat. You could even kill him!

This may sound excessive until you realize that your attacker is trying to rape you, kill you, or cause you some very serious injury. It's not pleasant to contemplate this possibility, but in a crisis situation your primary objective is to survive, and the damage you *might* do to your attacker will be less than he would cheerfully do to you! Remember that you did not make this person attack you: It was his choice, and if your attacker is a professional predator he has already factored in the risk of his being injured or killed.

Striking Techniques

When the subject is closing in on you, he won't just move toward you in a straight line. A study of the dynamics of assault reveals that an attacker does a lot of bobbing and weaving to get past your defenses. This means that the assailant's face, which is the *primary* target for the defensive keychain, is moving around a lot. As with the personal defense spray, hitting the target without training is more difficult than you might imagine.

Hitting the eyes, nose, and mouth of this moving target can be done reflexively as long as you're using proper striking techniques. Striking techniques are initiated from either the loaded or the ready position. The "secret" of striking the attacker is that wherever his face goes, the keys go. Remember, the target is the attacker's face.

After the initial training, you should practice your skill techniques on a daily basis for a minute or so until you're comfortable with the techniques. Once you're trained, you can perform repetitions of the technique using a mental visualization of the attacker's movements, or practice in dream simulations while asleep, which we will be discussing in more detail later this step under "Creative Visualization and Dream Practice."

There are five primary striking techniques for you to learn and practice. Like the spray patterns, these "gross-motor movements" are very much of the *Karate Kid* "wax on, wax off" school, and each one is based on movements that you've already performed thousands of times. They are what we refer to as *double-tap* movements, since each movement allows repeated strikes at your assailant by virtue of the multiple passes of the keys past his face as the defensive keychain is swung in repeated movements.

Horizontal Sweep

If the attacker is moving from side-to-side as he tries to come in at you, follow and strike his face with your keys by swinging the defensive keychain in a side-to-side sweeping motion, left to right or right to left. Remember, the assailant's mouth, nose, and eyes are the targets.

Vertical Sweep

If the attacker is trying to elude your defense by squatting or ducking down, follow and strike his face by swinging the defensive keychain in a down-and-up vertical sweeping motion.

Diagonal Sweep

Swing the defensive keychain in a 45-degree downward arc toward your reaction side from the loaded position, or up and around and then down from the ready position, striking your attacker in the center of the face with your keys. Swing the keys in a 45-degree upward arc toward your weapon side as a follow-up to a downward strike, or around and up from the ready position, striking at the center of the face.

Straight Thrust

Drive the keyring end into the center of your attacker's throat. You'll need to tip your fist down, your thumb at the top, to accomplish this. A straight thrust can be done from any position.

Criss-Cross Sweep

If the attacker is making diagonal movements, follow and strike his face with a criss-cross movement, trying to slash the letter X into the attacker's face with your keys.

Combination Strikes

Since you must continue defending yourself until the attack has ceased, it may be necessary to perform combination strikes until you are able to escape. The most common of these will be a series of downward or diagonal sweeps to the face followed by a straight thrust.

If Grabbed from Behind

If grabbed from behind in a choke hold or a bear-hug, the defensive keychain will be very helpful. If grabbed in a bear-hug, reach down and pull the defensive keychain from your waistband.

Jam either end into the back of your captor's hand as hard as you can, using both hands if necessary. This will cause intense pain—and possibly break some of the small bones in his hand—which should make him let go. Escape if you can, or pivot and strike your attacker and then escape.

If you are being choked from behind, turn your head so that your neck is toward his elbow. Pull the defensive keychain from your waistband and jab the end as hard a you can into his face, using both hands if necessary. The pain should make him let go. Escape if you can, or pivot and strike your attacker and then escape.

Defensive Keychain Training Simulations

You have been learning how to carry the defensive keychain and how to strike the assailant. Now you need to practice so that the proper responses will be so burned into you that you do them under stress without thinking.

Becoming proficient in the striking techniques will require you to perform the following simulations slowly at first, gradually building up speed, intensity, and complexity.

We recommend that when you practice, you pad your keys with cloth or paper, and then use duct tape around the padding. You'll need to practice where there is enough room to swing your keychain without hitting anyone or anything.

Two movements will help you strike harder. First, rotate your hips in the direction of your strikes, so that your entire body weight is behind the blow. Second, simultaneously sink down a bit and then uncoil upward when you do an upward strike, coil your body downward when you do a downward strike, or step-and-drag forward slightly when you do a thrust. This will also help put all your body weight behind each blow.

Level 1 Simulations

Practice moving into the ready and loaded positions—as discussed earlier in this "Using the Defensive Keychain" section under "Basic Positions") from the three basic stances (conversational, ready, and defensive—as discussed in Step 4 in the "Physical Skills for Self-Defense" section under "Stationary Stances"). Practice moving into each of these positions at least 50 times. The defensive keychain should be in your weapon hand, keys at the thumb end of your fist.

Next, exit the kill zone by "getting off the track," moving to the side as if avoiding a rushing attacker. Next, perform each of the three striking techniques in the air slowly and rhythmically. Give appropriate loud, repetitive verbal commands as you practice. Since you're doing three things at once (moving aside, striking, and yelling), start slowly and work up to a faster pace.

Perform each single direction movement until you are comfortable, first slowly for form, then faster, and finally at full speed and power, each time integrating moving aside and yelling.

When you're comfortable with the single-direction techniques, move to combination techniques and practice these in the same way until you're comfortable with them.

Level 2 Simulations

Making sure that the keys are padded, find a vertical object to strike. This could be a tree, a pole, a heavy punching bag, a mattress, or anything that can be struck without damage. Perform each of the three single-direction striking techniques against the striking surface, visualizing your attacker. When you are comfortable with this, add in the combination strikes.

Give appropriate loud, repetitive verbal commands and move "off the track," so that all three actions take place simultaneously.

Actually striking something will provide you with more realism and positive feedback about how much power and shock you can generate. You'll be glad you're not the one getting hit.

Level 3 Simulations

Level 3 simulations require the help of a training partner carrying a padded bag or some other surface that can safely be struck, who moves in to assault you from various attack positions and with varying movements. It is very important that you and your partner choreograph what is being done so that neither of you gets hurt!

As your partner moves in toward you, holding the striking surface *well in front of the face*, follow and strike the striking surface with the padded keys while verbalizing and moving to the side. You can tell right away by feel if you're not hitting the target. Start with the single-direction strikes and move to the combination techniques.

Be very careful when working with a partner. There is no need for these movements to be done fast, or in a manner which can get out of control!

As you become proficient at striking the surface representing the face moving in toward you, continue integrating your patterns of movement to get away and run for help. As always, integrate verbal stunning with your physical movements.

Dynamic Simulations

Finally, you should make up scenarios, little plays in which you stage a scene where things escalate until you are attacked and must defend yourself. These may be practiced *very carefully* with padded keys and a partner, or in your imagination. Think through how you would apply the defensive keychain to each of the scenarios used earlier with a personal defense spray.

Creative Visualization and Dream Practice

Not all practice has to be physical. You can also visualize in your mind, or in your dreams, scenarios in which you defend yourself. The advantage is that if you make a mistake, you can stop the visualization, go back, and then do it over again until it's perfect. As far as your body is concerned, as long as you do *some* physical practice, these nonphysical sessions will be "thought of" as real, and will help to establish the neural pathways required for reflexive action to take place.

Dreams are an effective way to learn since you can create scenarios that are virtually indistinguishable from reality—with the exception that you can stop and replay them until their outcome is the way you want, and that you can be frightened in a dream, but not hurt. To learn to control your dreams, you can read *Creative Dreaming* by Patricia Garfield (New York: Ballantine, 1985).

During a dynamic simulation, creative visualization, or dream practice you should feel some of the psycho-physiological effects of a violent confrontation that are discussed next.

Psycho-Physiological Aspects of Violent Confrontations

Between conditions Orange and Red (which we discussed in Step 3 under "Awareness") a host of psycho-physiological reactions start taking place within the body. These unavoidable reactions are caused by the fight-or-flight reflex. They start when the body dumps adrenalin and other hormones into the blood stream, causing both heart rate and blood pressure to rise. Blood is channeled to the internal organs from the extremities (which is why people go pale under extreme stress).

On the positive side, some of these reactions increase your body strength and give you a much-enhanced tolerance to pain. Both of these can be a great help in a violent confrontation.

On the negative side, other reactions are less helpful. Fine-motor coordination diminishes, first in the reaction hand, then in the weapon hand, then in the legs. This means that you will be able to perform gross-motor skills such as the five spray patterns and striking techniques, but not fine-motor skills requiring fine coordination or small hand movements, such as multiple short sprays.

On a psychological level you may perceive a distortion of time (called *tachypsychia*), where time is remembered as passing quickly (usually if you were unprepared) or slowly (usually if you were prepared). Because of this it's *very unwise* to discuss the specifics of time immediately after a confrontation. Since time was distorted for you, whatever you say will probably be wrong. If you're wrong about the timing of the incident, and end up in court, you will likely hear opposing counsel say something like "You lied about how long the alleged attack lasted. What other lies are you telling?"

Fortunately, you don't have to be unreasonably specific. It's acceptable to say "I was attacked. It happened very fast and was very confusing. I know I was in danger, but I'm not sure I can be accurate while I'm this upset." Then shut up!

You may also suffer from *tunnel vision*, where your brain allows you to focus only on the immediate danger. If your attacker has a weapon, you may find yourself seeing only the weapon. This does two things: First, you're likely to become so fixated on the immediate danger that you won't see other dangers—or even people or things that might be of aid. You must train yourself to turn your head and look around you.

Second, as with a telephoto lens, objects—and even people—can seem larger than life: A small attacker might appear to be a much larger person, a small knife might appear to be a huge knife, a small gun might appear to be a cannon, and a long distance may appear to be a short distance. This means any definitive descriptions you give of weapons or attackers right after the incident are probably wrong. Again, don't discuss details prematurely. It's acceptable (and true) to respond to a question like "How close were they?" with an honest "Close enough to hurt me!"

Remember also that when the light is low, colors are distorted: The gray car, truck, or jacket you saw might really have been blue or red.

Auditory exclusion is much like tunnel vision in that the brain filters out sounds it doesn't consider important. You might not hear your attacker's accomplice, or the person coming to your aid. As you might expect, what you recall hearing may not be what others recall hearing.

The moral of all this is that you should be very careful about what you say after an incident: Be aware that since much of what you remember may not be exactly correct in its specifics, you should stick to the most elemental facts until the adrenalin is no longer pumping through your system. Talk as little as necessary.

And Don't Forget Our Goal

Remember that our primary goal is to keep you from being attacked in the first place. Only if you can't avoid a confrontation do you need to put into practice your strategies, techniques, and tactics to break away from an attack and get help. If you are attacked and successfully get away, you need to run to help and protection, then call the police.

How to Survive the Aftermath of a Violent Confrontation

IMMEDIATELY NOTIFY THE POLICE
OF THE ATTACK

STEP 6
IMMEDIATELY NOTIFY THE POLICE
OF THE ATTACK

If you are on the receiving end of an assault, it's important that you notify the appropriate law enforcement agency as quickly as possible. Your primary goal here is to protect your status as a law-abiding citizen.[14]

From the police viewpoint, there are three possible participants associated with any incident: The *complainant* (the one who was attacked and files the complaint), the *defendant* (commonly referred to as the suspect), and the *witness*.

As a general rule the first party to contact the police about an incident is the complainant. You want to be the complainant, since there is a near-universal impression that the complainant is the good guy and the defendant is the bad guy. If you don't notify the police, it allows your assailant to assume the role of complainant. The following

---

14. An important secondary reason for calling the police right away is to help them catch your attacker as quickly as possible. This will help get a predator off the streets, which is good for both you and your community. More importantly, your active participation in the process will help you recover from the stress of having been attacked.

scenario provides just one example of how this kind of misrepresentation can occur:

You have been confronted by a potential attacker. You have followed the rules and have successfully used an emergency safety tool on the subject, who is now bent over, dealing with the effects of your defense. You decide that there's no more danger, and so you leave. Because you weren't hurt, because you are shaken by the incident, and because you don't want to even think about what happened, you don't call the police. Unbeknownst to you, the incident was observed by a witness looking out his second-floor window.

The witness was unable to hear any conversation between you and your attacker. Your assailant had his back to the window, and the witness could not observe any physical actions on your assailant's part. The activity observed by the witness was that two people met on the sidewalk, and one disabled the other and then left the area. The witness calls 911 and requests both police and medical services for the subject doubled over on the sidewalk.

What story do you think your attacker will tell the police and medical personnel? What story will the witness tell the police and medical personnel? You should be aware that in most cases your assailant will make up a story for the police which will have you playing the role of the aggressor. In one recent incident, the attacker claimed that his

140

intended prey made sexual solicitations, and, when rebuffed, attacked. The assailant thus claimed that he was merely defending himself.

This scenario is only intended to stimulate your thought processes and to help serve as an example of why we urge you to call the police anytime you're assaulted. There are many "what ifs" associated with these types of incidents, and we don't pretend to have all the answers. However, we hope this provides some insight about why you should contact the police.

What the Police Will Ask You

Law enforcement officers are trained professionals whose job is to apprehend criminals. They will be addressing two primary areas during the initial interview stage. The first is: Has there been a crime committed, and by whom?

The following are some of the questions you may be asked:

- Where were you coming from?
- Is this part of your normal route?
- How soon before the attack did you notice the assailant?
- At what point did you realize you were going to be attacked?
- What do you think drew the attacker's attention to you?

- What did the assailant say?

- What was your response?

- Was he was bigger, stronger, younger, in a group, a male if you are a female?

- Were you injured, exhausted, or knocked to the ground?

- Where any weapons actually displayed? If yes, what kind?

- Did he appear, either from knowing him or from observation of his actions, to be a boxer, a martial artist, or otherwise more dangerous than might be expected.

- Do you know, or have you ever before seen, your attacker?

- What did your attacker look like? (Start with a general description and then begin at the top and work down with the specifics. Example: "A white male about 20 years of age, weighing about 175 pounds, with long dark hair and no hat, no glasses, and appearing clean-shaven." Start practicing now, as you move through your daily activities, how to describe people. Learn to zero in on unique behaviors or mannerisms, and different manners of dress.)

- In what direction did the assailant flee?

- Did you notice the assailant interacting with anyone else?

This is not intended to be an all-inclusive list—it merely represents some of the general questions that would be asked. If there are any injuries to either you or the offender, these would also be addressed, along with any other unusual variables associated with the incident.

The second area the police will be questioning you about is: Are you carrying the emergency safety tool in compliance with the applicable laws? If you have followed our advice to check out your local laws, you should have no problem with this.

What You Should Ask the Police

No matter how upset or shaken you are after an incident, there are some questions you should ask the police. Start with the reporting officer's name. This may seem foolish at first, but more often than not this point is overlooked and several days after an incident the complainant is trying to locate "the officer who took my report." The larger the police department, the harder it will be to locate the unknown officer.

You should find out if the reporting officer is doing any follow-up work concerning the case, or if it will be transferred to some specialized group, like the detective unit. You also want to know the case number being used.

Additional questions would include: Who do you contact—and how—if you think of more information concerning the case? How do you get copies of the reports? Are there any court appearances you need to be aware of? How do you contact the prosecutor and the court?

You should also ask what other actions you can take to help apprehend your assailant. Actively aiding the police in apprehending your assailant is not just to help them. It's also to help you deal positively with the fact that you have been violently assaulted and that your personal space has been violated.

If You are Sexually Assaulted

While any assault is a violation, sexual assault is particularly traumatic and full of uncomfortable social overtones. Because of this, a sexual assault survivor can be so confused and embarrassed that she or he will, more often than not, want to delay calling the police, or not want to call them at all.

Although this is natural, it's not a good idea for three reasons. First, delay increases the time it takes for the emotional and psychological healing process to begin. Second, delay reduces the likelihood of there being physical evidence which can be used by the police and prosecution against your attacker. Finally, it is an unfortunate truth that there will be people who won't believe your charges, particularly if your assailant denies them. Sadly, the longer you delay, the more that people who don't understand the psychological pressures involved will question why you didn't call the police sooner, and whether anything even happened. You don't need this additional grief. Call the police immediately.

Physical evidence will be needed, so no matter how distasteful it is, do *not* change clothes, douche, or clean up. Don't throw away anything that might be evidence, and don't take any medication. Bring a change of clothes with you, as the clothes you were wearing may be needed by the prosecution for evidence.

In the past some police officers had a less-than-sensitive approach to those who had been sexually assaulted. This is changing, and you should expect—and demand—to be treated with dignity, sensitivity, and respect.

Do You Need an Attorney?

The last issue in this section is the question of whether or not *you* need an attorney. We must make it clear that we are not attorneys and do not provide legal advice. So the only one who can answer this question is you.

The judicial system does not provide you, as the complainant, with an attorney. If someone is arrested and charged based on your complaint, the

145

state provides a prosecutor, and a defense attorney for the defendant, but nobody for you. It would be wise at least to discuss the matter with your own attorney, or one in whom you feel confident. There are too many variables in the law for you to risk going unadvised, especially if you were injured or if your attacker suffered any injuries during the attack and sues you.

If you do hire an attorney, try to find one who has experience in this area: Just because an attorney can close on a mortgage doesn't mean he or she knows the criminal justice scene. And you must speak with other clients so you can figure out if the attorney's any good: Justice Renquist is reputed to have said that half the attorneys who appear before the Supreme Court are unprepared. If we assume that it is the best of the best who make it to the Supreme Court, it is a safe guess that things are much worse on a local level.

Don't feel that you are embarrassing or insulting your potential attorney by doing this investigation: Since there is so much at stake once you get involved with the justice system, you must be as careful in selecting an attorney as you would be in selecting a heart or brain surgeon. Someone once said that there are two equally important parts to self defense: In the street and in the courtroom. If you choose your attorney wrongly, your experience with the criminal justice system could be as traumatic as your experience with the criminal.

146

DEAL WITH THE POST-TRAUMATIC STRESS
OF BEING ASSAULTED

STEP 7
DEAL WITH THE POST-TRAUMATIC STRESS OF BEING ASSAULTED

Being violently assaulted is strange and disorienting. The reality of dealing with someone who is trying to hurt you is frightening on every level. The raw intensity of the experience makes it hard to believe that it really happened. But it *does* happen, and you *do* survive. Remember, there are no winners in a confrontation, only survivors.

If you are violently assaulted you may suffer no after effects, or the trauma sustained may affect you for a long time. Remembering the attack won't be a good thing, but it doesn't have to dominate your thoughts or your life.

The one thing on which everyone agrees is that you should not try to bury the memory of what happened. Instead, it is recommended that you deal with it directly. Studies have shown that how you deal with the aftermath of a violent confrontation depends on how you feel about what you did during the incident, how others feel about what you did, and on whether you are aware of the effects of post-violence trauma. But, no matter what happened or what others say, it's important that you understand that it wasn't your fault, and that you did the right thing in defending yourself.

If you feel you did your best, you're likely to recover more quickly and with fewer effects than if you feel you were unprepared. If you receive support from your friends, family, and peers, you'll be better off.

You may be worse off if you find yourself criticized in the newspaper, or are wrongly told by others that the incident was your fault ("You should have known better than to be there," "You must have encouraged it somehow," etc.), or if you are sued by your attacker.

Being aware of the possible effects of post-violence trauma can create a certain *inoculation effect*, allowing you to recognize that you're having a problem, and therefore be more able to deal with it. Merely reading this book and others like it starts the inoculation effect.

Individuals who have been violently assaulted may experience at least some of the most common potential after effects of a traumatic incident:

- *Sleep disturbance* is quite common. You may suffer from an "adrenalin hangover": While your body is quick to dump adrenalin into the blood stream, it's not so quick to use it up. You want to sleep, but the residual chemicals simply won't let you do so. You may also suffer, later, from insomnia, disturbing dreams, or dreams involving generalized helplessness caused by a natural preoccupation with the traumatic event.

- *Isolation* is a two-headed problem. On the one side, friends and family may not know what to say to you, or feel you want to be alone, and keep away. On the other side, you may feel uncomfortable around people who don't understand what you've been through, and keep them away. It's important that you force yourself to continue with as normal a social life as possible. If you feel a need to be alone, it is probably a sign that you need to be with others.

- You may additionally suffer from generalized *depression*. Incredibly, you may not even connect being depressed with the incident.

- *Intrusive recurrent recollections* of the incident may drift into your thoughts, or you may even be caught in a closed-loop recollection of the incident, where you replay the assault over and over again in your mind with the same unsatisfactory outcome.

- You may find yourself having *flashbacks* to the incident, especially in circumstances that remind you of the incident, particularly in conjunction with alcohol consumption.

- A similar starting event may trigger *anxiety*.

- You may develop an *exaggerated startle response*, or *hyper-vigilance*. Checking the doors and windows before you go to bed is prudent vigilance; checking them a dozen times during the night is hyper-vigilance.

151

- You may face the *aggression/avoidance syndrome*, where you behave in an inappropriately ferocious manner in mildly confrontational situations that should be nonthreatening: You appear to try to provoke a confrontation so you can win it. Or you may back away from normal yet nonthreatening conflicts.

- You may have a temporary increase in *compulsive behaviors*, such as eating or drinking too much, gambling, or whatever.

- If you are wrongly castigated by the press or by other people, you may suffer from *logorrhea.* This is "diarrhea of the mouth," where you feel a compulsion to discuss the incident and justify yourself in public. Don't! You should speak with your attorney and, if appropriate, with your therapist or counselor, and nobody else.

Note that some people suffer none of these after effects. You, yourself, may suffer none, some, or all. The important thing is to be aware that they *might* happen to you, and be able to recognize the symptoms. It's not abnormal to have a few problems in readjusting after an assault, but you can and will deal with these problems.

It's also important to realize that while it's normal to experience some post-violence trauma after an incident, if the primary symptoms are still going strong a month or more after the incident, you may have moved into *post-violence stress disorder*, which is a problem that definitely requires professional attention.

Even though we have received some training in counseling those who have experienced traumatic events, the topic is not one that can be dealt with in this book. We do know, however, that by preparing yourself mentally, physically, and emotionally for a violent assault, you will definitely deal with the post-violence trauma better than if you had not been prepared. So be a survivor! Actively prepare yourself for the reality of what can happen and you'll be better off for it.

If you are violently assaulted, we recommend that you seek out experts who are trained to help you deal with your trauma. You can contact some or all of the following to find help:

- Your local law enforcement agency, to find out to whom they send officers after a shooting incident.

- Someone from the clergy—priest, pastor, minister, rabbi, religious counselor.

- Social worker.

- Psychologist or psychiatrist.

- Counselor, therapist, or therapy group.

CONCLUSION

Painful and sad as it is to have to deal with even the *concept* of people assaulting other people, we have tried to provide you with a set of tools and techniques that can help you and your loved ones achieve personal safety.

In the best case, with care and a bit of luck you and yours will avoid confrontation, and go through life with great awareness and joy. In the worst case we hope you will survive a confrontation, and go through life with an even greater awareness, joy, and appreciation for life.

While we can honestly say that we understand the dynamics of avoiding, dealing with, and surviving the aftermath of a violent confrontation, what we've shared is not the only possible plan of action, and nothing will work for everyone 100% of the time. We encourage you to read about and actively participate in other training concepts and programs: If you can learn even one useful thing, it's time well spent.

Congratulate yourself! By taking to heart the information in this book you have changed your life by working to control your own destiny!

Thank you for listening to us and hearing us out.

God bless you, and stay safe!

ACKNOWLEDGMENTS

We would like to thank publicly the following individuals, organizations, and publications for their knowledge, training, help, and assistance in making this book possible. Where an individual is named, the organization is given for identification purposes only.

*Aerko International (Mike Dallett),
    Fort Lauderdale, Fla.
Dan Allender, *The Wounded Heart*
    (Colorado Springs, Colo.: Navpress, 1990).
* Craig W. Andersen, Clarkstown P.D.,
    New City, N.Y.
* Massad Ayoob, Lethal Force Institute,
    Concord, N.H.
D. F. Bach, illustrator, New York, N.Y.
Frederick E. Bidgood (who suggested expand-
    ing the civilian version of the ASR Instructors
    Council personal defense spray program into
    this program), copy editor, New York, N.Y.
Bruce Cameron, *Law and Order*, Wilmette, Ill.
Donna Chaiet, prePARE, Inc. (IMPACT^{sm}),
    New York, N.Y.
Arthur Cohen, Target Consultants International
    Ltd., East Meadow, N.Y.

General Guidance on Personal Security Measures (New Scotland Yard, London).

Larry Crabb, The Institute of Biblical Counseling, Colorado Springs, Colo.

Joanna Cumberland, J.B. Cumberland and Associates, New York, N.Y.

* Defense Technology Corp. of America (Chuck Oblich), Rock Creek, Ohio.

Peter DiVasto, University of New Mexico, Albuquerque, N.M.

Greg Epilone, Alison Graphics, Inc., New York, N.Y.

* Federal Laboratories (Ken Blakey), Saltsburg, Pa.

* Joe Ferrera, Southfield P. D., Southfield, Mich.

Carol Gilligan, *In a Different Voice* (Cambridge, Mass.: Harvard University Press, 1982).

Mark Greenglass, Ambassador Alarm, Brookline, Mass.

Robert Grodin, TTI Group, Ltd., Morrisville, Pa.

* Elliott Grollman, Federal Protective Service, Washington, D.C.

* David B. Haas, Washington Township P.D., Sewell, N.J.

*Larry Hahn, Waterloo P.D., Waterloo, Iowa.

Phil Hanum, Shoreline Community College, Seattle, Wash.

* David Hemond, Pawtucket P.D., Pawtucket, R.I.

Ken Howard, photographer, San Diego, Calif.

156

* Walter Hyzer (who came up with the name *The Seven Steps to Personal Safety*), independent use-of-force training consultant, Cumming, Ga.
* Martin Imwalle, Arlington P.D., Arlington, Texas.
Naomi J. Isaacs, New York, N.Y.
* William A. Jackson, Nassau County P.D., Mineola, N.Y.
C. Ray Jeffery, *Crime Prevention Through Environmental Design* (Beverly Hills, Calif.: Sage Publications, Inc., 1971).
Brian Keenan, *An Evil Cradling* (New York, N.Y.: Viking Penguin, 1992).
Josh Konecky, Proof Perfect, Inc., New York, N.Y.
* Jerry Konrad, independent use-of-force training consultant, Gainsville, Fla.
* Kansas City Regional Police Academy (Hugh Mills), Kansas City, Mo.
Gary Klugiewicz, Milwaukee County Sheriff's Department, Milwaukee, Wisc.
Pat Kogan, Pat Kogan Productions, New York, N.Y.
* Lethal Force Institute (Massad Ayoob), Concord, N.H.
Michael Levine, *Guerrilla P.R.* (New York: Harper Collins Publishing, Inc., 1983).
Jim Lindell, National Law Enforcement Training Center, Kansas City, Mo.

Robert Lindsey, Jefferson Parish President's
Office, Gretna, La.
* Jerry Lucas, TTI Group, Ltd., Morrisville, Pa.
* John Ludvigson, Newport Beach P.D.,
Newport Beach, Calif.
* Charles J. Mader (who contributed much of
Step 6), Bloomingdale P.D.,Bloomingdale, Ill.
Robert A. Marino, New York, N.Y.
* Earby Markham, Port City Investigation &
Security Services, Inc., Mobile, Ala.
Jerry McCarthy, Wheaton, Md.
* William J. McCarthy (who coined the term
aerosol subject restraint), For Life Manage-
ment, Indianapolis, Ind.
Tom McCoig, independent use-of-force training
consultant, Oak Ridge, Tenn.
John Negus, New York P. D., New York, N.Y.
Oscar Newman, *Defensible Space* (New York:
MacMillan Publishing Co., Inc., 1973).
Catherine Nicodemo, designer/illustrator,
New York, N.Y.
* North Mississippi Law Enforcement Training
Center (Mark Dunston), Tupolo, Miss.
Kevin Parsons, Kevin Parsons and Associates,
Appleton, Wisc.
* Curt Price, Fort Lauderdale P.D.,
Fort Lauderdale, Fla.
* Pro-Aer (Michael Carl), New York, N.Y.
Charles Remsberg, Calibre Press, Inc.,
Northbrook, Ill.

Joseph Scurto, DeSantis Holster and Leather, Inc., New Hyde Park, N.Y.

* Charles Sczuroski, Jr., Pawtucket P.D., Pawtucket, R.I.

Stephen Selwyn, Napanoch, N.Y.

Bruce Siddle, PPCT Management Systems, Inc., Waterloo, Ill.

* Smith & Wesson Academy (Bert DuVernay), Springfield, Mass.

* State University of New York (Bill Dunn), Albany, N.Y.

Terry Smith, Monadnock Training Council, Monadnock Lifetime Products, Inc., Fitzwilliam, N.H.

The Company of Women, Nyack, N.Y.

Jeffrey R. Snyder, "A Nation of Cowards," The Public Interest, Fall, 1993.

* Anthony Spector, Minneapolis Park Police, Minneapolis, Minn.

* Jack Strenges, Palm Beach Sheriff's Office, West Palm Beach, Fla.

Alice Thompson, line editor, New York, N.Y.

* John Vazquez, Elizabeth P.D., Elizabeth, N.J.

Tom Ward, FBI, Portland, Ore.

Bay Wasserman, New York, N.Y.

*Tim White, U. S. Army Military Police, Fort Levenworth, Kans.

Robert Wilson, Palm Beach Sheriff's Office, West Palm Beach, Fla.

APPENDIX A:
THE SEVEN STEPS
TO PERSONAL SAFETY

Step 1
Be aware of your vulnerability.

Step 2
Mentally commit to doing everything you can
to stay safe.

Step 3
Be aware of your environment
and take reasonable precautions.

Step 4
Get away by creating and maintaining distance.

Step 5
Stop the assault and then get away.

Step 6
Immediately notify law enforcement authorities
of the attack.

Step 7
Deal with the post-traumatic stress
of being assaulted.

160

APPENDIX B:
TACTICAL WARM-UPS

Before you participate in any physical practice you need to perform a *tactical warm-up*, which involves a series of heating and stretching movements. While you won't have time for this when attacked, a tactical warm-up is important to prevent training injuries.

You should consult a physician before beginning any exercise program, including this one.

Benefits of Tactical Warm-ups

There are two major benefits you get from a tactical warm-up:

First, your performance is improved because when you gradually increase your physical speed and intensity, heart rate, respiration, and circulation, the temperature of your entire body increases, which makes your muscular/skeletal anatomy more elastic and resilient against tears and breaks. Your muscles, tendons, and joints increase their ranges of motion, making you more efficient in your movements.

And second, your chances of injury are prevented or reduced, because once your body is

161

heated and stretched out it has more flex and give than when it was cold, stiff, and rigid.

Heating Phase

The heating phase involves a series of light rhythmic upper- and lower-body movements that relate to personal defense techniques, and should last about five minutes. The following movements are a good example of how to heat your body up:

Marching in Place: Swing your arms as you lift your knees. Allow your heels to bottom out so as to take the strain away from the calf muscle and the Achilles tendon. This heats your hips, thighs, knees, calves, and ankles.

Alternating Jabs and Punches: From a wide and deep foot position, perform punching movements to heat your frontal shoulders, chest, and arms. Mentally visualize confronting an assailant striking him as he comes toward you.

Alternating Leg Kicks: From a wide and deep foot position, perform alternating foot kicks toward the legs and thighs of your imaginary attacker. This will heat your abdominal and lower-back muscles, your hips, thighs, knees, and your ankles.

Reverse Forearms: Perform alternating forearm strikes toward an assailant who has gotten you in a bear-hug from behind. These movements will

162

heat the back of your shoulders, your upper and lower back, and the muscles over your rib cage.

Alternating Knees: From a good deep and wide foot position, perform alternating knee strikes to the lower abdomen of the attacker. Try to make pointed spears with your knees. This heats the gluteus muscles of your buttocks, your side abdominal muscles, and your thighs and knees.

Forward Forearms: From a deep and wide foot position, perform alternating forearm strikes to the chest and abdomen of the attacker. As you strike, make sure to hold your fists to your chest as you extend your forearms out away from your body as far as possible. This movement heats your frontal shoulders, chest, and side abdominal muscles.

Shoulder Shrugs: Rotate your shoulders up and forward to heat your shoulder muscles and joints. Then reverse and rotate them up and back.

Elbow Extensions: Extend your arms straight out in front of you. Then bring your hands straight back to your shoulders and press them back out. This movement heats your elbow joints.

Wrist Rotations: Extend your arms in front of you and rotate your wrists inward, then outward. This heats your lower forearms and wrists.

Hand Compressions: Extend your arms straight out in front of you, then begin closing your hands into fists and opening them. This movement will heat the muscles of your hands.

Stretching Phase

Once you have completed the heating phase, you're ready for the stretching phase.

To achieve the best results in your stretching, hold each stretch for at least 20 seconds as you breathe freely through your nose and mouth. Try to avoid holding your breath as this causes your blood pressure to rise unnecessarily.

Stretching should last about five minutes.

Reach-to-the-Sky: From a good deep and wide foot position, cup your hands together in front of you and then reach straight up as high as you can. This movement stretches the lower and upper back, shoulders, chest, arms, and abdomen.

Bent-over Shoulder: From a wide and deep foot position, cup your hands together behind your back and bend over so that your upper body is parallel to the ground. Then lift your hands off your back straight up as high as you can without forcing the stretch. This movement stretches the chest, shoulders, and upper back.

Rotational Forearm: From a wide and deep foot position, make a fist with each hand, bring your knuckles together, and tuck them into your chest with your elbows splayed wide. Rotate your entire upper body to the left and then to the right as you maintain a stationary foot position. This stretches your shoulder muscles over the rib cage, side abdominals, and your upper and lower back.

Vertical Side Bend: From a wide and deep foot position, put your left hand on your left thigh and extend your right hand straight up. While maintaining a stationary foot position, bend over sideways to your left. Change your hand positions and then bend sideways to your right. This movement stretches your shoulders, rib cage, side abdominals, and upper and lower back, and secondarily stretches your arms.

Modified Toe Touch: From a wide and deep foot position, bend your knees and lower your body. Put your right hand on your left toe, extend your left hand straight up in the air, and look up at your hand. Reverse position, with your left hand on your right toe, and look up at your right hand. This movement stretches your chest, shoulders, and upper back.

Groin Stretch: From a wide straddle base foot position (as if you're riding a horse), shift your entire body to your right while keeping at least a 90-degree bend in your knees. Then shift your body to your left. This movement stretches your inner groin, thigh, knee, calf, and ankle.

Stretch Squat: With your feet placed shoulder width apart and your toes pointed slightly outward, squat straight down, having your knees follow the outward angle of your toes. Keep your head up and your back arched as you squat down and try to keep your heels flat. This stretches your lower back, the gluteus muscles of your buttocks, the hips, and the upper frontal thighs.

Bent-over Hamstring: With your feet placed shoulder width apart, bend forward at the waist, squatting down and placing your fingertips on the ground. Now extend your buttocks up in the air as high as you can without forcing. This stretches your lower back and the back of your thighs.

Tune-ups

Whenever you take a break from your training or activity and become inactive, even if it's only for a few minutes, it's a good idea to reheat your body. We call this reheating a "tune-up." To perform a tune-up requires that you participate in just the heating phase of the tactical warm-up. The tune-up should last from three to five minutes.

Cool-downs

After practicing, it's important to go through a *cool-down* period, where you do simple movements such as walking in place while swinging your arms lightly, while your blood pressure moves back to a normal range. While a warm-up is designed to protect your muscles, a cool-down allows your dilated blood vessels to contract to normal size. Without a cool-down it's possible for your blood pressure to fall rapidly, causing fainting or worse.

APPENDIX C:
ABOUT THE AUTHORS

Richard B. Isaacs is a charter member of the Aerosol Subject Restraint Instructors Council, the American Society for Law Enforcement Trainers, and the Tactical Response Association. He is a member of the American Academy for Professional Law Enforcement and the American Society for Industrial Security. A student of Aikido and a competitive shooter, he is a certified instructor in a wide range of law enforcement less-than-lethal emergency safety tools and techniques.

Richard came across aerosol subject restraints in 1986, when they were virtually unknown. His company began marketing them in 1987, and introduced them to the law enforcement community at the 1988 conference of the American Society of Law Enforcement Trainers. Based primarily on his efforts, ASRs gained widespread recognition within the law enforcement community.

Because Richard was concerned that there were no programs for police officers in the use of personal defense sprays, his company developed the first course in the use of personal defense sprays, introduced at the 1989 conference of the American Society of Law Enforcement Trainers, and now offered through the ASR Instructors Council.

167

In 1990 Richard recognized a need for increased personal safety as well as widening use of personal defense sprays by the public. He decided that the law enforcement personal defense spray program should be adapted for "civilian" use. In 1991 his company developed a civilian personal defense spray program based on its law enforcement program. It was introduced at the 1992 conference of the American Society of Law Enforcement Trainers, expanded in 1993 into the personal safety program presented in this book, and is now offered through the Center for Personal Defense Studies.

An Eagle Scout who served in the Peace Corps, Richard received his undergraduate degree from New York University and his Masters degree from Columbia University. He has a wide variety of outside interests and is a member of the Aircraft Owners and Pilots Association, la Confrérie de la Chaîne des Rôtisseurs, Mensa, and the National Rifle Association. He has been listed in *Who's Who in the East*, and in his spare time works on the Samaritans Suicide Help Line and as a supernumerary at the Metropolitan Opera.

Richard is currently a director of TTI Group, Ltd., a security consulting/risk management firm established to protect high-risk clients and augment their security by providing specialized training, executive protection, and crisis management for corporate, government, and private security.

168

Tim Powers has worked within the criminal justice system for over 16 years. He has held such positions as organized crime research analyst, prison sociologist, juvenile social worker, deputy sheriff, marshal, and chief of police.

Tim has simultaneously integrated academic training as well as practical experience from the fields of exercise physiology, kinesiology, bio- and body mechanics, and performance training into his research and experience in the criminal justice system.

Tim has designed and written training curricula, and has appeared on a number of national television programs as an expert on use-of-force techniques, tactics, and performance systems. He developed a course and produced a video training film called *Tactical Aerobics* which combines specific emergency services job tasks and motor performance skills with cardiovascular/respiratory endurance conditioning.

In addition to his position as executive director of the Fitness Institute for Police, Fire and Rescue, Inc., Tim has held positions as the director of training at the National Law Enforcement Training Center, a member of the national board of directors of Armament Systems & Procedures, Inc. (ASP Impact Weapons), and a member of the national board of directors of RISC Management System of Mechanics of Arrest.

Tim has presented over 325 seminars in the United States, Canada, Australia, and Europe, training over 52,000 people. He has trained personnel from many federal agencies including the FBI, Drug Enforcement Administration, Border Patrol, Department of Agriculture, Forestry Service, Treasury Department, Internal Revenue Service, Postal Service, Federal Law Enforcement Training Center, Coast Guard, and Army.